The EGG Book

See how baby animals hatch, step by step!

Contents

Author Robert Burton
Additional text Dr. S. James Reynolds
Original photography Jane Burton, Kim Taylor
Illustrator Ella Ginn

Project Editor Olivia Stanford
Designer Brandie Tully-Scott
US Senior Editor Shannon Beatty
US Editor Mindy Fichter
Project Picture Researcher Rituraj Singh
Managing Editors Marie Greenwood, Jonathan Melmoth
Managing Art Editor Diane Peyton Jones
Jacket Coordinator Magda Pszuk
Production Editor Dragana Puvacic
Senior Production Controller Ena Matagic
Publishing Director Sarah Larter

PREVIOUS MATERIAL
Editor Gillian Cooling
Designer Tina Robinson
Project Editor Mary Ling
Project Art Editor Helen Senior

Material in this publication was previously published in *Egg* (1994)

First American Edition, 2023
Published in the United States by DK Publishing
1745 Broadway, 20th Floor, New York, NY 10019

23 24 25 26 27 10 9 8 7 6 5 4 3 2
005–333017–Feb/2023

Consultant

Dr. S. James Reynolds is an Assistant Professor at the University of Birmingham and an expert on birds.

Important information

Remember never to touch eggs in the wild or disturb nesting animals. They can be very protective of their nests, so it's best to keep your distance.

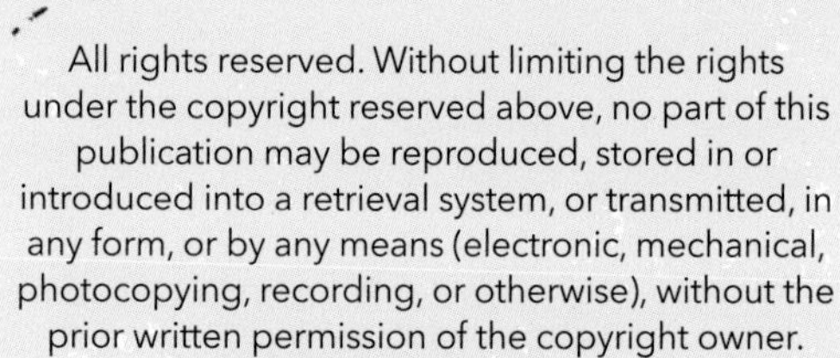

Published in Great Britain by Dorling Kindersley Limited

A catalog record for this book is available from the Library of Congress.
ISBN 978-0-7440-6996-9

DK books are available at special discounts when purchased in bulk for sales promotions, premiums, fund-raising, or educational use. For details, contact: DK Publishing Special Markets, 1745 Broadway, 20th Floor, New York, NY 10019
SpecialSales@dk.com

Printed and bound in China

For the curious
www.dk.com

This book was made with Forest Stewardship Council ™ certified paper—one small step in DK's commitment to a sustainable future.

For more information go to www.dk.com/our-green-pledge

What is an egg?

An egg is the first stage in the development of a baby animal. It is made by a female animal. All eggs develop in the same way. They start as a tiny speck that grows into the different parts of the animal's body. When people think of an egg, they usually think of a chicken egg—but there are many other kinds.

Color

Many bird eggs have brightly colored eggshells, which can be plain or speckled. Some have dull colors and patterns that make them difficult for predators to see. This is called camouflage.

This Japanese quail's nest shows how hard it can be to see well-camouflaged eggs in a nest.

Great tit egg

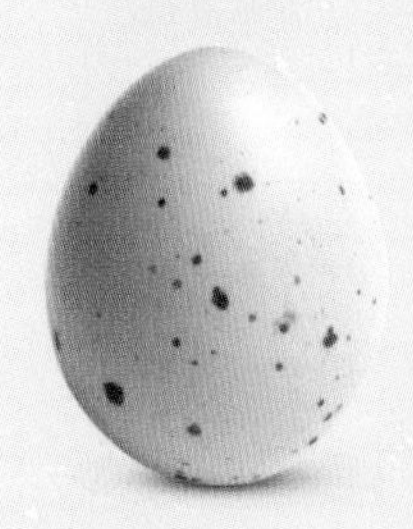

Song thrush egg

Dogfish egg case

Shape

Bird eggs are usually oval or pointed at one end. Other animals have eggs that are different shapes, such as spherical tortoise eggs or rectangular dogfish egg cases.

Leopard tortoise egg

Leopard gecko egg

Bird eggs can be dull, or shiny—like this emu egg.

Emu egg

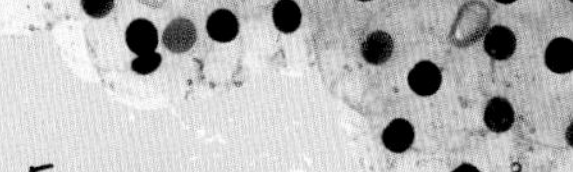

Frogspawn

Moorhen egg

Eggshells

Most animals' eggs are protected by a shell. Birds and insects lay eggs with hard shells. Snakes and some other animals lay eggs with soft shells. Frog eggs do not have a shell, but are protected by jelly instead.

Corn snake egg

Peregrine falcon egg

Size

Eggs range in size from tiny, such as those of insects, to very large, like those of an ostrich. The common ostrich lays the largest egg of any living bird. Animals that produce larger eggs usually lay smaller clutches than animals that produce smaller eggs.

The butterfly egg below is 100 times smaller than an ostrich egg.

Swallowtail butterfly egg

Common starling egg

Black swan egg

Common ostrich egg

Birds

Bird eggs have a hard, chalky eggshell. Inside the egg, there is a thick layer of egg white, or albumen, around the yellow yolk. Birds are the only animals that sit on their eggs to keep them warm.

Great crested newt

Who has eggs?

Every kind of animal produces eggs and some lay them. The baby animals, called embryos, develop inside the eggs and hatch out when ready. Other animals, including most mammals, do not lay their eggs. Instead, their eggs develop inside the mother's body, and are eventually born as babies.

Insects

Insects lay their eggs singly or in clusters, often hidden under leaves. Most insect eggs hatch into wormlike larvae, which later change shape completely to become adults. Others hatch as nymphs, which slowly grow into winged adults.

Mollusks

Mollusks, such as slugs and scallops, are a large group of invertebrates. Slugs and snails lay their hard-shelled, round eggs in holes in damp ground. Aquatic mollusks, including scallops, release tiny eggs that hatch into swimming larvae.

Common frog

Amphibians

Most amphibian eggs are laid in freshwater, often covered in a jelly that provides protection and warmth. Amphibians lay large numbers of eggs because many are eaten by other animals, such as fish, before they hatch.

Goldfish

Fish

Fish eggs are laid in water and have soft shells. They hatch into baby fish, called larvae. A few kinds of fish give birth to babies. Like amphibians, fish lay a lot of eggs in case some are eaten.

Leopard tortoise

Reptiles

Reptiles lay their eggs on land. The eggs have waterproof eggshells that can be hard or leathery. They hatch into miniature adults. Even sea reptiles, such as turtles, must return to land to lay their eggs.

Corn snake

Short-beaked echidna

Mammals

Very few mammals lay eggs, but even those that do still produce milk to feed their young, just like all other mammals. Egg-laying mammals include the platypus and the echidna, which live only in Australia and on the island of New Guinea.

Nesting

Nests are places where animals lay their eggs and raise their young. A male and female animal usually pair up to defend the area, or territory, where they will build their nest. The nests that birds make come in many different forms. Some are simple hollows scraped into the ground, while others are intricate baskets made by carefully weaving plants together.

Which comes first? To produce an egg, you need a chicken, but to have a chicken, you need an egg! Female chickens, called hens, start laying eggs when they are around 12 months old.

Fertilizing the eggs

A male chicken is called a rooster. When the rooster mates with the hen, the eggs inside the hen are fertilized by his sperm cells. This needs to happen before a chick can start to develop inside an egg.

Preparing the nest

Before the hen starts to lay her eggs, she makes a scrape in the ground with her beak and feet. She pulls twigs, feathers, hay, and leaves up around her. The hen lays 7–15 eggs in the nest.

Laying the eggs

The female lays one egg every day until she has a full clutch. She does not start to incubate them until the last egg of the clutch is laid. Because of this, all the eggs start to develop and hatch at the same time.

Types of nests

It is not just birds that build nests. Many types of animals that lay eggs create a safe place in which their clutch can develop. Some fish blow bubbles to create nests of foam, and alligators carefully construct nests of grass and mud.

Long-tailed tits build beautifully camouflaged nests. Both the male and female work together to create an enclosed ball from moss, spiders' webs, and lichens.

Barn swallow parents make cup-shaped nests out of mud collected from puddles. The nests are built high up, often on the beams of roofs, where the chicks are safe.

Male paradise fish blow bubbles of air to make a nest of foam at the water's surface. When the female lays her eggs, they float upward into the bubble nest.

A female American alligator builds her huge nest by herself. She creates a mound of plants and mud, then digs a chamber in which to lay her eggs.

This chicken egg has just been laid. The embryo has already started to grow. It develops from the small disk of cells on the surface of the yolk.

2

A network of blood vessels has spread over the yolk, and the heart has started to develop. The blood carries nutrients from the yolk to the embryo.

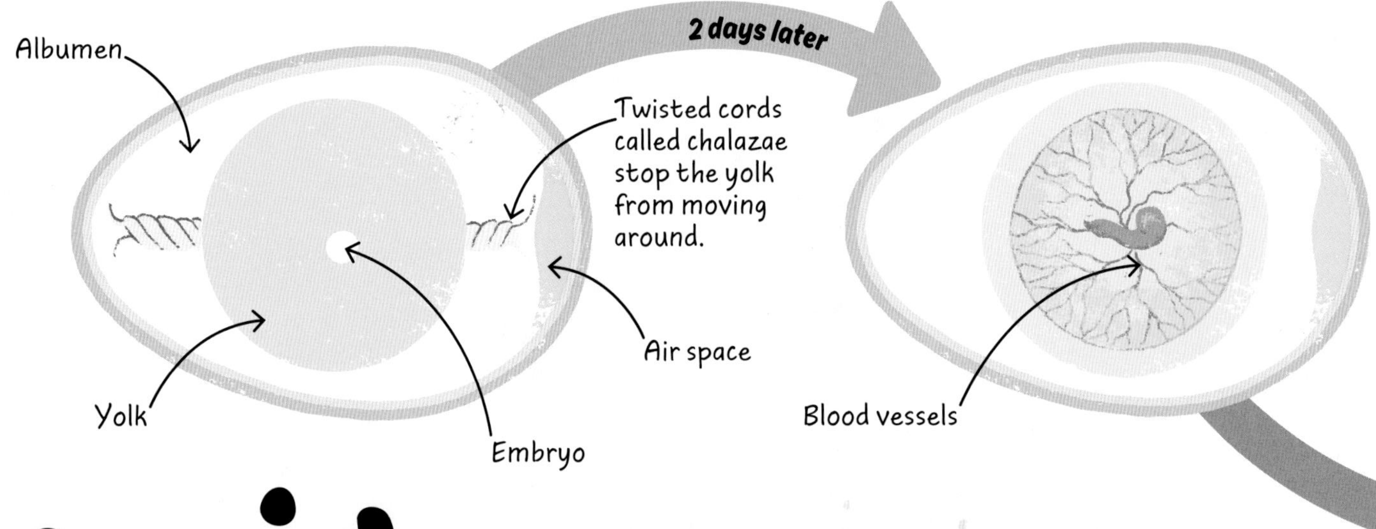

Inside an egg

Every egg starts as a single cell in its mother's body. It is fertilized by another cell called a sperm from the father. Once the egg is fertilized, it starts to develop. The first stages of development are the same in most animals. The egg cell divides into two new cells, which then divide again. Cell division continues and the developing animal, called an embryo, forms and starts to look more like its parents.

Development of a chicken egg

It takes around 24 hours for a chicken to produce an egg. This happens inside a special tube called an oviduct. A newly laid egg does not have a chick inside it. The egg must be incubated for the chick to develop.

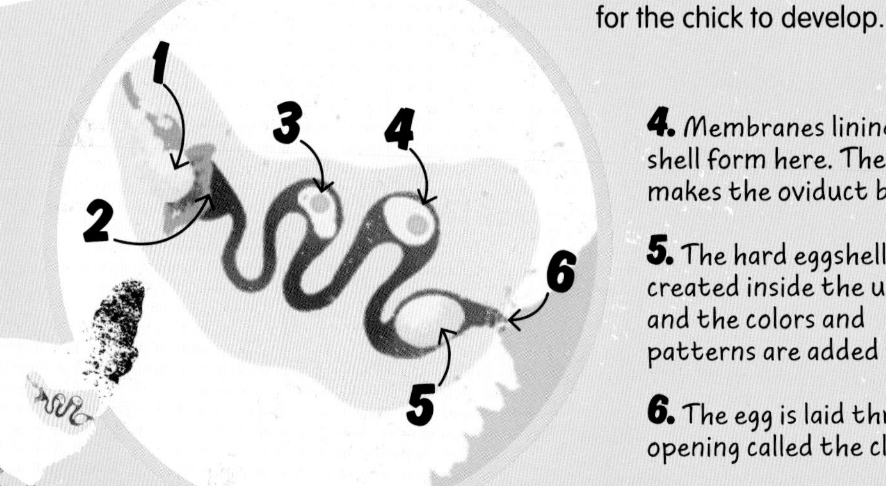

1. The egg cell, which is mostly yolk, is released from the ovary into the oviduct.

2. Fertilization occurs here.

3. Most of the egg white, or albumen, is laid down here.

4. Membranes lining the shell form here. The egg makes the oviduct bulge.

5. The hard eggshell is created inside the uterus, and the colors and patterns are added to it.

6. The egg is laid through an opening called the cloaca.

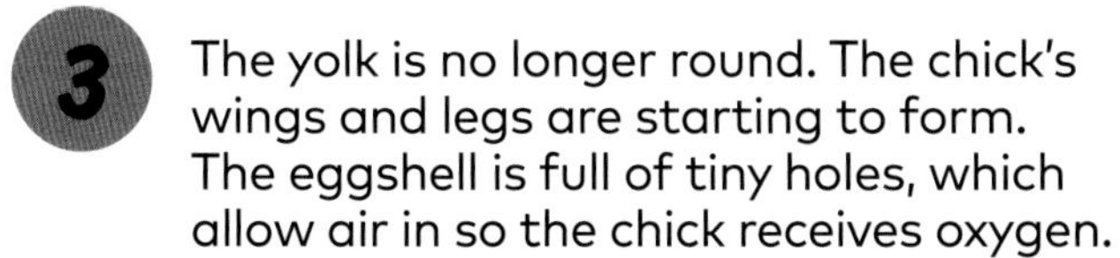

The yolk is no longer round. The chick's wings and legs are starting to form. The eggshell is full of tiny holes, which allow air in so the chick receives oxygen.

The embryo is beginning to look like a bird. The beak is forming, and tiny spots show where the feathers will grow. The waste sac is now visible.

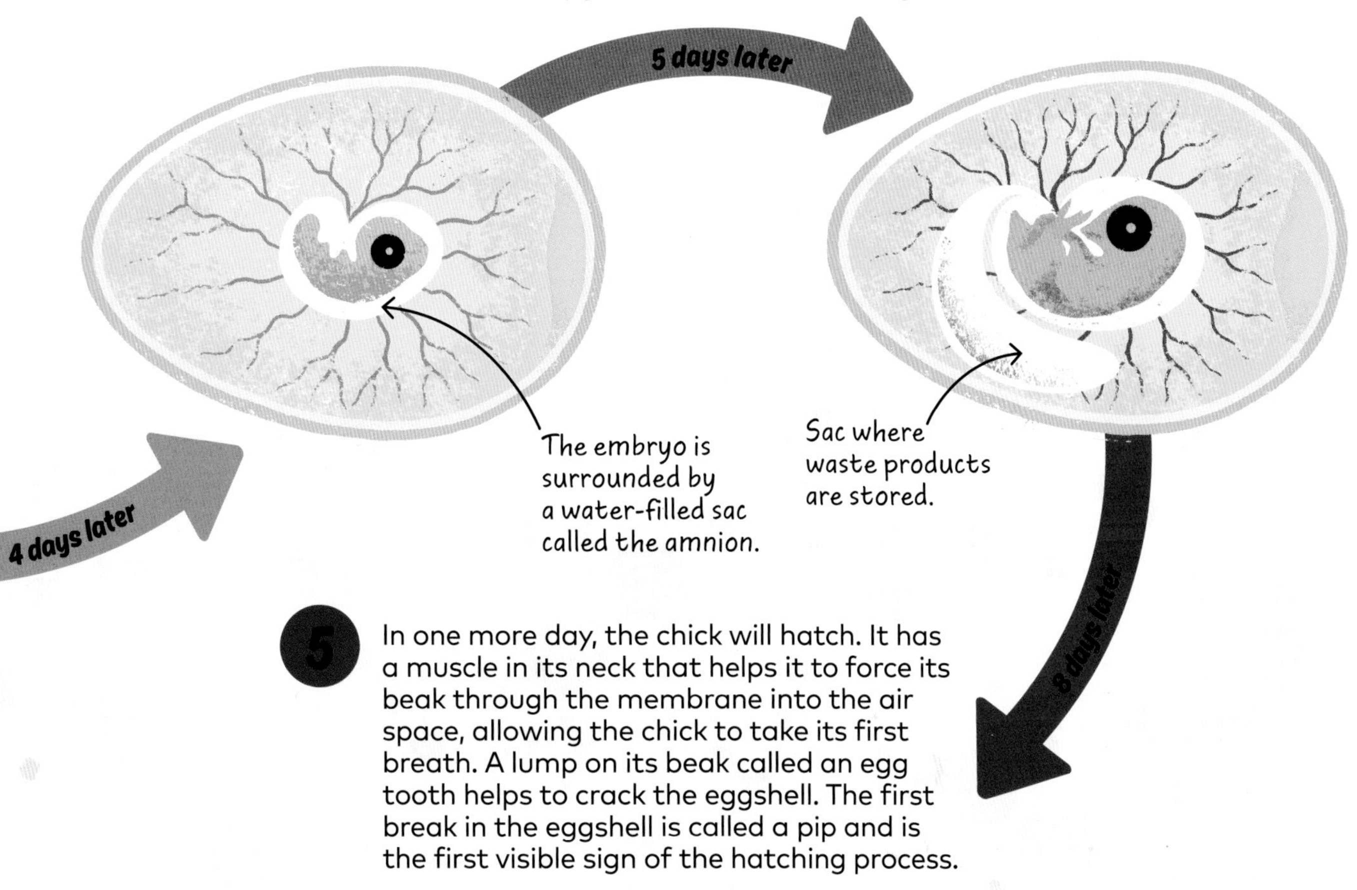

5

In one more day, the chick will hatch. It has a muscle in its neck that helps it to force its beak through the membrane into the air space, allowing the chick to take its first breath. A lump on its beak called an egg tooth helps to crack the eggshell. The first break in the eggshell is called a pip and is the first visible sign of the hatching process.

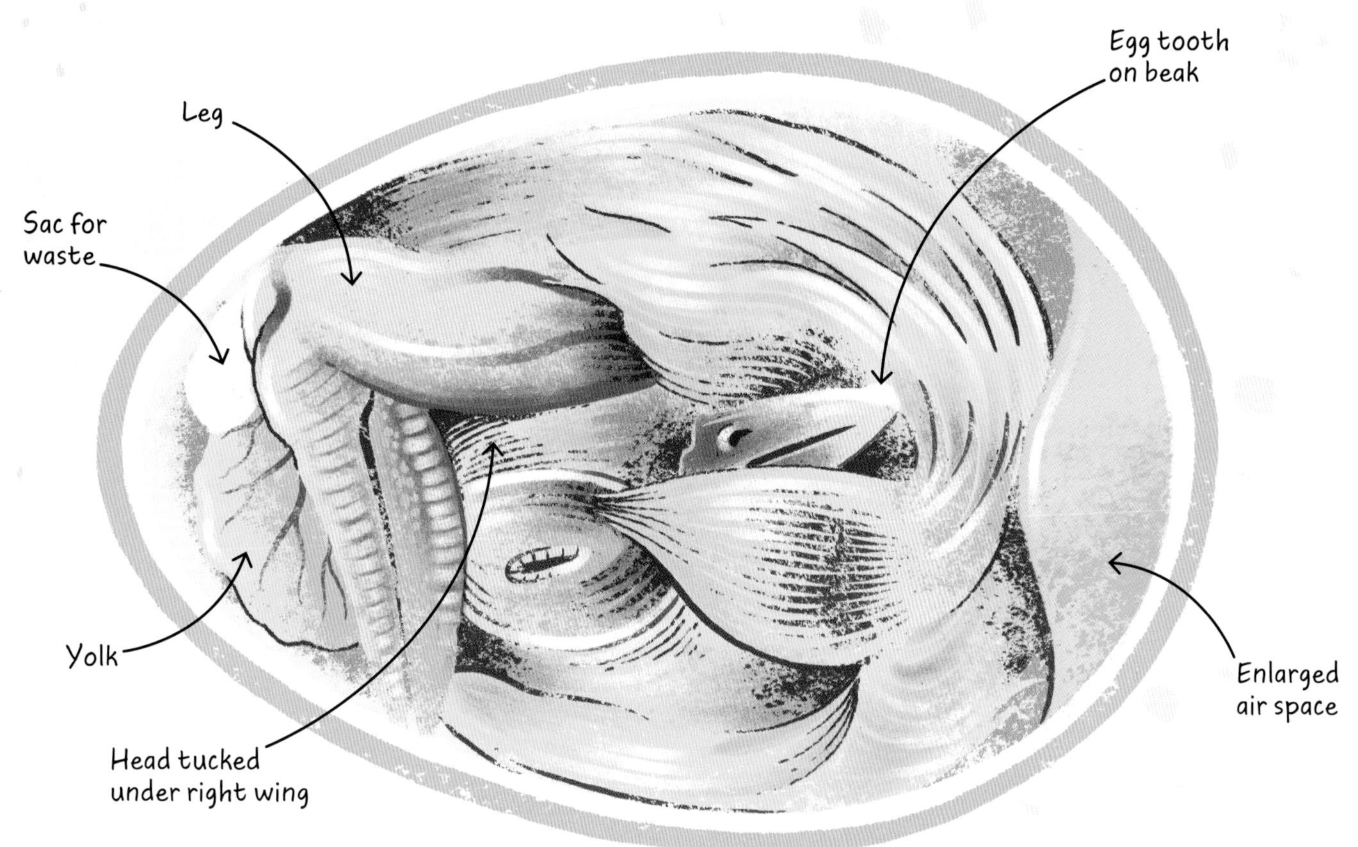

1 Common ostrich eggs are rounded and cream-colored. The eggshell is 0.08 in (2 mm) thick, making it very tough.

2 days, 1 hour, and 40 minutes later

2 The baby ostrich uses its strong beak to hammer a hole in the eggshell. Because its neck is curled around, the hole is made near the middle of the egg.

The chick begins to breathe air freely as soon as the eggshell is pipped.

1 hour and 20 minutes later

Common ostrich

Common ostriches live in the dry savannas of Africa. They are the largest birds in the world, and also lay the largest eggs. The female lays up to 12 eggs, which can weigh 4 lb (2 kg) each. The female incubates the eggs during the day, and the male incubates them at night. The chicks are normally ready to hatch after 42 days.

Big family

Several females may mate with the same male and then lay their eggs in one nest. After they hatch, the chicks are guarded by just one pair of adults. Chicks from several nests may join together and form a group called a crèche that can contain up to 100 chicks!

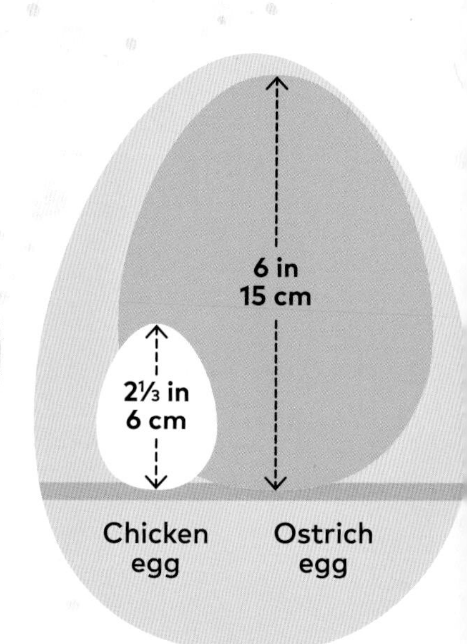

3
Unlike most chicks, the ostrich chick has no egg tooth to help it break the eggshell. Instead, its sturdy legs press hard to push chunks of shell away.
As the chick kicks, large pieces of eggshell fall off, like this one.
25 minutes later
4
The ostrich chick has been hatching for more than 50 hours now. The hole the chick has made is almost large enough for it to squeeze through.
5 minutes later
5
Suddenly, the chick bursts out. It needs to rest after finally breaking free. Its downy feathers are still wet, but they soon dry out and become fluffy.
6
The chick is now three days old. It is several days before the chick can stand securely. Then, it will leave the nest and run around with the other chicks. The chicks look for their own food, such as grasses, leaves, flowers, and seeds.
An ostrich has only two toes on each foot.

Roman goose

The Roman goose is a small domestic goose. Most domestic geese, including the Roman goose, are descended from wild greylag geese. A Roman goose lays around six creamy white eggs in each clutch, and up to 45 eggs in a year. These are incubated by the female for 28 days while the male, called the gander, keeps guard over the nest.

1 Inside the egg, the baby goose, or gosling, starts to move more than usual. Soon it will poke a hole in its eggshell.

16 hours and 55 minutes later

2 After a circle of holes has been pecked, the gosling starts to push. The cap begins to break off the eggshell.

10 minutes later

3 The gosling is almost out of its egg. It is curled up at first, and not yet able to straighten its neck.

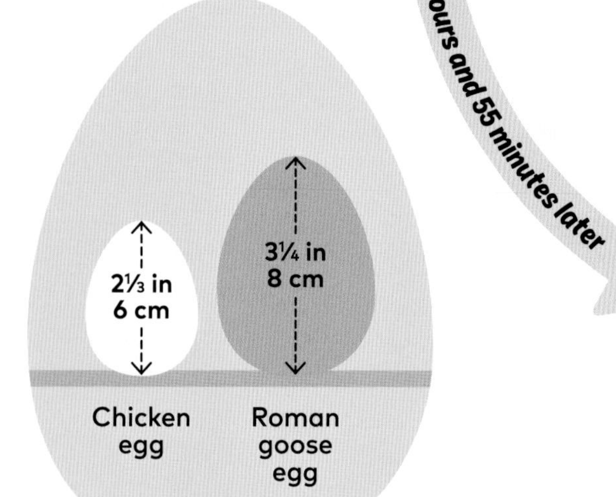

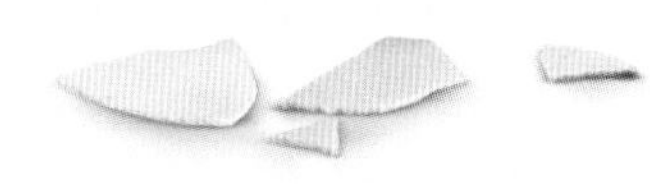

Tufted goose

The Roman goose is said to be one of the oldest farmyard geese in the world. It has been bred in Italy for at least 2,000 years. Some have a tuft of feathers on their head.

4 After more than 17 hours, the gosling is finally out of the egg. It rests for a while, before finally sitting up.

The gosling's feathers are wet, but they will dry to become yellow and fluffy.

5 The gosling is now one day old. It can open its eyes and has large, strong legs when it hatches. After two or three days, it leaves the nest and runs after its parents. They will lead it to a place where it can find food by itself.

Moorhen

The moorhen lives in many parts of the world. It builds its nest from a pile of plants at the edge of a river or pond. The nest is built high enough to keep the eggs out of the water—sometimes it even floats. The female moorhen lays two clutches of five to nine eggs each year, which are incubated for 20 days.

2 minutes later

1 Moorhen eggs are pale and speckled. Soon the chick will pip the eggshell, starting at the blunt end of the egg.

1 day and 35 minutes later

2 Once the chick has completed a circle of holes, it pushes hard to make a gap in the eggshell.

2 minutes later

3 The chick has almost pushed its way out of the egg. It breathes air through the space it has made in the eggshell.

$2\frac{1}{3}$ in
6 cm

2 in
5 cm

Chicken egg

Moorhen egg

4 After more than a day's effort, the chick bursts out of the egg. Its feathers are still damp, but it can open its eyes.

The chick rests before it finally breaks free.

Growing up

After around 50 days, the chicks are able to take care of themselves. At first, their feathers are brown. Moorhen chicks from the first clutch of eggs often help their parents to look after the chicks from the second clutch.

5 The chick is now one day old. Moorhen chicks are soon strong enough to run and swim after their parents. When the weather is cold and wet, the chicks shelter under the adults' feathers. They stick close to their parents and each other when looking for food, in case of danger.

Wing with claw

The chick has no webbing between its toes. This causes it to swim jerkily.

Bird eggs

Bird eggs are all made of the same materials, including a substance called calcium that makes their shells hard. However, the eggs can look very different. They might be big, small, rounded, pointed, plain, patterned, white, or colorful. Most birds lay one egg per day until the clutch is complete, but clutch sizes can vary from one egg to twenty or more.

South island takahē

This flightless waterbird lives only in New Zealand where it is endangered. It lays just two blue-and-brown spotted eggs in a clutch.

Southern brown kiwi

Flightless kiwis live in New Zealand. They lay a single huge egg that is the biggest compared to their body size of any bird.

Emu

Emus are the second largest bird on the planet. They lay dark green eggs that turn black, and eventually white, if left in sunlight.

Common murre

Murres nest on cliffs in groups containing thousands of birds. The blunt end of each egg stays clean above the muck surrounding it.

Domestic chicken

Domestic chickens are descended from red jungle fowl in the wild. Usually chickens lay white or brown eggs, although some are pink, green, or blue.

Guira cuckoo

Unlike other cuckoos, which lay their eggs in the nests of other types of birds, female guira cuckoos often share nests with each other.

American robin

American robins lay blue eggs. This helps them to know if a cowbird has sneakily laid its own pale, speckled egg in their nest!

Melanesian megapode

This bird buries its eggs to keep them warm, sometimes using the heat of volcanic ground to incubate its clutch. Its chicks can fly within a day.

Elegant crested tinamou

Tinamous nest on the ground in Central and South America. They produce bright, glossy eggs that are as shiny as glazed pots.

Golden plover

The eggs of the golden plover have brown splotches, which help to camouflage them. These birds make their nests on the ground.

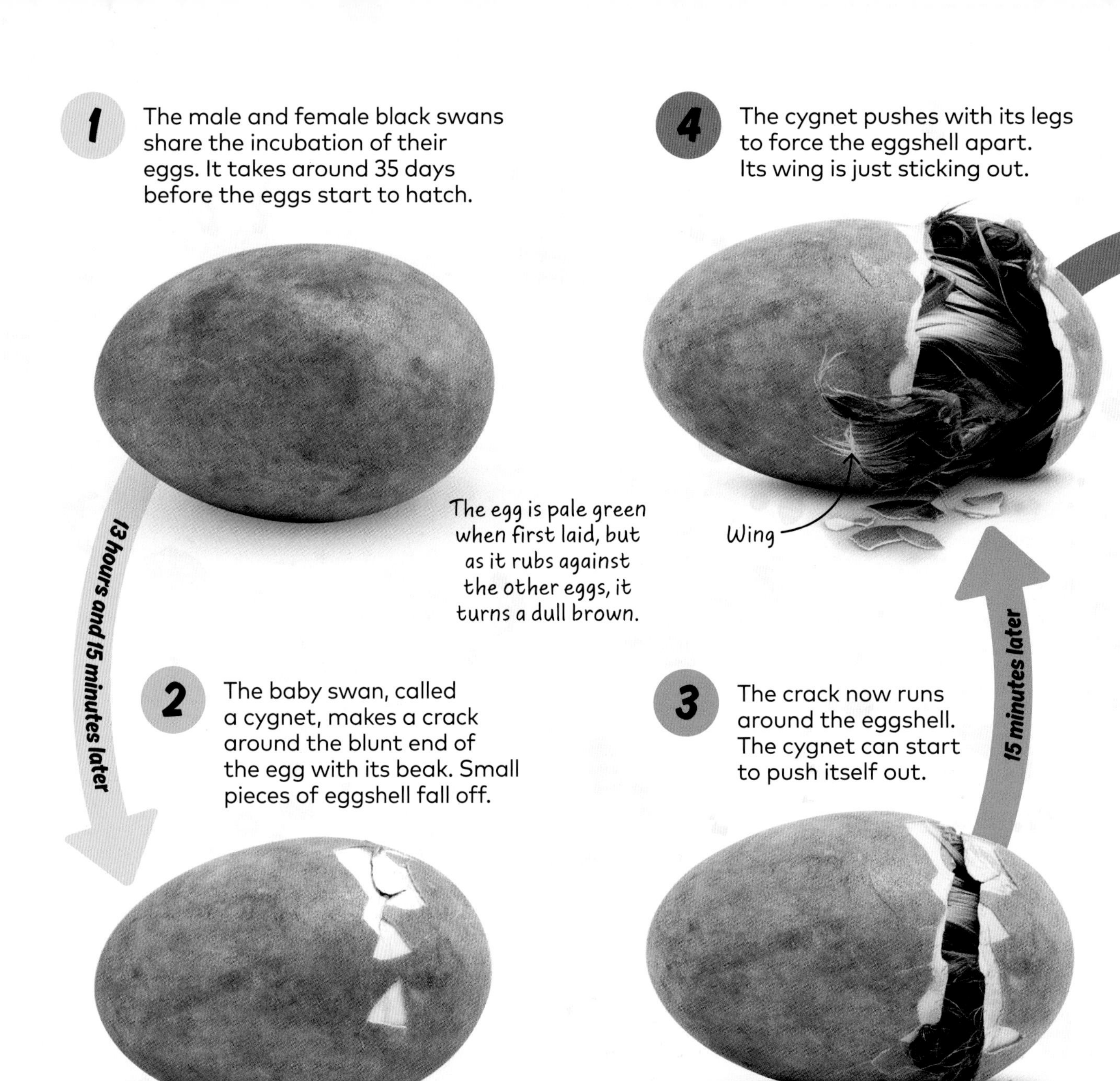

Black swan

The black swan lives in Australia and New Zealand. It also lives in parks in other countries. Its nest is made from a heap of water plants, and can be up to 3 ft (1 m) across. Both parents gather the plants and pile them up, and the female lines the nest with down. She then lays five or six eggs, which hatch in five to six weeks.

Safe cygnets

The oldest cygnets leave the nest with one parent before the other eggs have hatched. Several families of cygnets may live on the same pond. The chicks are safer from predators in a large group.

15 minutes later

The cygnet looks around now that it has left the safety of its egg.

5 The cygnet is resting after spending most of the day breaking open its eggshell. Its mother will keep it warm until its down becomes dry and fluffy.

6 This cygnet is now two days old. It is soon able to leave the nest. Swans hatch with their eyes open, a lot of fluffy feathers, and the ability to run quickly. The chick's gray feathers turn black by the end of its first year.

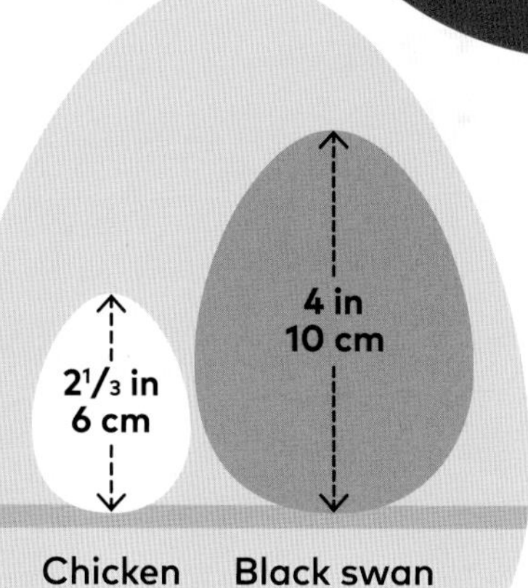

Muscovy duck

Muscovy ducks come from South America, where they were tamed before being taken to other countries. Wild Muscovy ducks live in ponds and streams in forests, and feed on water plants and animals. They are good at perching on branches and make their nests in holes in tree trunks. The female lays eight to nine eggs that hatch in five weeks.

1 The eggshell is in two pieces. This happens around 24 hours after the egg was first pipped by the baby chick.

10 minutes later

2 The duckling is pushing the top off the blunt end of the egg. It pushes with the back of its neck and head.

2 minutes later

3 With a few more pushes, the duckling is almost out of the egg.

Chicken egg	Muscovy duck egg
2⅓ in 6 cm	2⅓ in 6 cm

5 The duckling is now one day old. Once the chicks have hatched, they must jump down from their nest in the trees. They then follow their mother to water.

4 The duckling cheeps as it hatches out of the egg. Its mother may call back to it.

Cozy nest

Like many ducks, the Muscovy duck lines its nest with fluffy feathers, called down. The female has plucked these from her own chest. The down provides a soft and warm bed for the ducklings.

1 The golden pheasant chick makes the first hole in the eggshell. This takes place around 23 days after the egg was laid.

2 The chick makes a ring of holes that join to form a long split. Its damp feathers can be seen inside the egg.

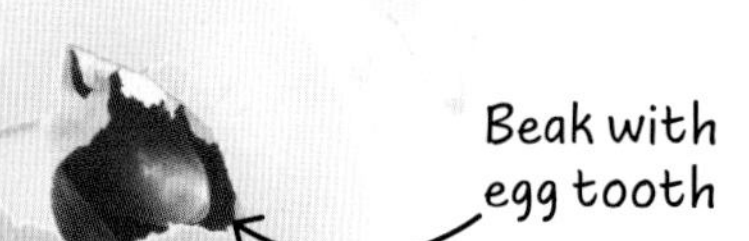

Beak with egg tooth

10 minutes later

Golden pheasant

The golden pheasant lives in the bamboo forests of China. The male has rainbow-colored feathers, and the female is brown. The female lays 5 to 12 eggs in a clutch, which she incubates while the male finds food. The nest is a simple, shallow hollow in the ground, like a saucer.

Colorful display

Male golden pheasants are named for their yellow back and head, but they also have red, green, and blue feathers. A female chooses a male to mate with partially based on the brightness of his feathers.

3 The little chick uses its feet to help push itself out of the egg. Its body is still curled around to fit inside the egg.

4 After more than five hours, the chick is almost free from the egg. It will soon be able to stand.

5 These one-day-old golden pheasant chicks hatched out of their eggs at around the same time. They are not yet ready to leave the nest. They will wriggle under their mother's body to keep warm.

Japanese quail

The Japanese quail is a relative of the pheasant. The male's call can be easily heard, but these birds are hard to spot. The female lays around 10 eggs in a shallow nest scraped into the soil, often among crops that hide it from view. The eggs have dark patches that help to camouflage them in their nest.

1 The quail egg starts to hatch. This takes place around 16 days after it was laid.

1 hour and 17 minutes later

2 The chick makes a crack around the blunt end of the egg.

13 minutes later

Staying hidden

The Japanese quail's patterned feathers help to camouflage it, in a similar way to its eggs' patches. This is especially important for the female when sitting on the nest, since it keeps her safe from predators.

3 The end of the egg opens like a lid as the chick pushes itself out. The chick's pink beak can now be seen.

4 The chick is out of the egg. The chicks from the same nest cheep to each other from inside their eggs, and all hatch at the same time.

5 This chick is now two days old and not much bigger than a bumblebee. Its fuzzy feathers have dark patches like its parents to help to hide it in the grass.

Aylesbury duck

The Aylesbury duck is a white farmyard duck bred from the wild mallard. It is named after the town of Aylesbury in England, which is famous for its ducks. The female lays 10 eggs in each clutch, and up to 100 eggs in a year. She builds the nest, and incubates the eggs for 28 days. The male does not help to rear his young.

4 With big kicks, the duckling struggles out of the egg. The chick is exhausted from opening the eggshell.

After more than 20 hours, the chick has emerged. It rests while its down dries.

5 The duckling is now two days old. After hatching, the duckling leaves the nest forever. Oil from its mother's feathers, and later from a gland near its tail, makes its down waterproof. The mother duck leads her hungry brood to the water to look for food.

Incubators

Breeders of chickens and ducks can copy how adult birds incubate their eggs. The eggs are placed on trays in units called incubators, which keep the eggs at the right temperature until they hatch.

Cunning cuckoos

In this dunnock nest, one egg is different from the rest. A common cuckoo has laid its white egg here deliberately, so that when it hatches the dunnock parents will have the job of feeding its young instead.

1 It is already 20 hours since the baby penguin pipped the first hole. It rests, then turns inside the egg, pecking until a ring of holes forms.

The baby penguin has made three separate holes in the eggshell.

2 days, 2 hours, and 20 minutes later

2 The chick continues to turn around inside the egg and make more holes. Eventually, it makes a jagged cut right around the egg.

2 hours and 20 minutes later

3 There is just enough room for the chick to push with its wings and kick its feet. It also tries to straighten its neck. As it does, the crack opens up even more.

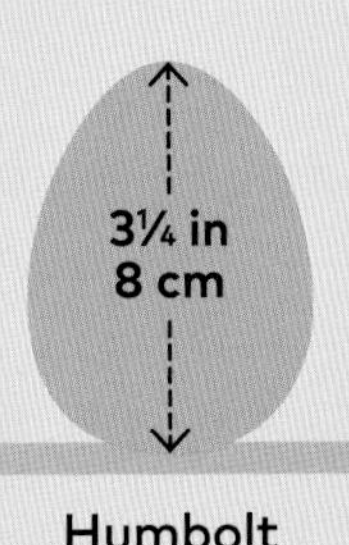

Humboldt penguin

Penguins can't fly, but they have sleek bodies that are well adapted for swimming. Humboldt penguins live in the sea off the coasts of Peru and Chile, and nest on islands. They come ashore twice a year to lay their eggs. Females lay two eggs in each clutch, and both parents share the incubating, which takes 28 days.

4 Suddenly, the chick's head appears. The lid of the eggshell flips open and the front of the chick's body comes out.

After more than three days of effort, the chick has finally hatched out of the egg.

5 The chick is now three days old. It is fed fish regularly by its parents. After seven weeks, it will have grown its waterproof feathers, and at ten weeks it swims out to sea.

The chick is covered in velvety, gray down.

6 The penguin is now two years old. As adults, penguins usually return to the place where they hatched to lay their own clutch of eggs.

The adult penguin has waterproof feathers that help to keep it warm and dry.

Cool burrows

Humboldt penguins do not like hot weather. The females lay their eggs beneath rocky ledges or in burrows in the ground where the parents are shaded from the sun.

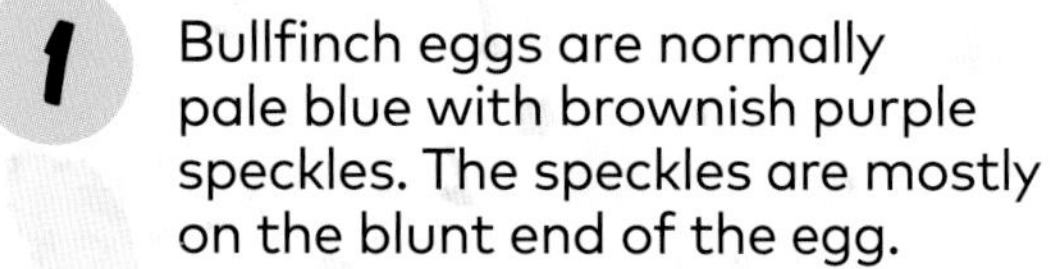

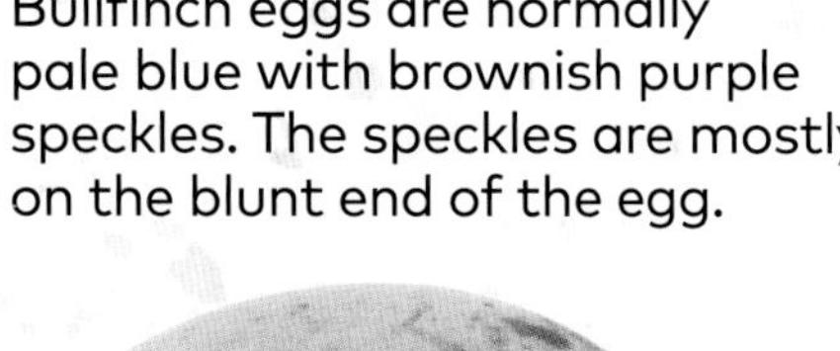

1 Bullfinch eggs are normally pale blue with brownish purple speckles. The speckles are mostly on the blunt end of the egg.

14 hours and 30 minutes later

2 The chick has been working hard and has almost completed a ring of holes around the eggshell.

5 minutes later

3 The chick pushes to free itself from its tight-fitting eggshell. Its pink skin can be seen through the crack.

1 minute later

4 With a few last pushes, the baby bird is almost free from the egg. Its damp feathers are stuck together.

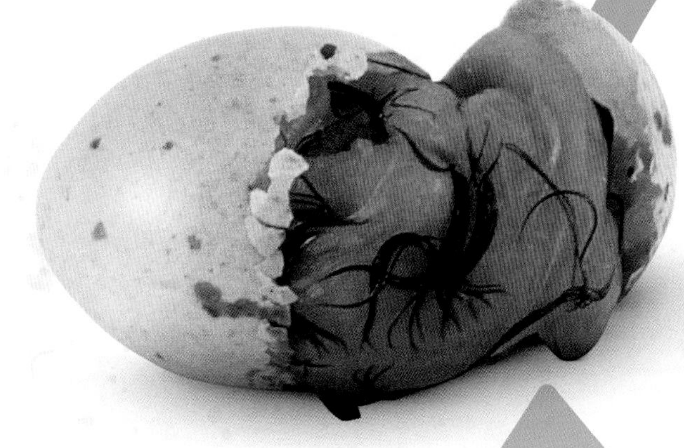

Bullfinch

The bullfinch lives in woods and hedges. The female lays up to six eggs, two to three times a year. She incubates the eggs for 12 to 14 days. The adults eat mostly seeds and buds, but they feed insects to their young to provide a richer diet. When nesting, both the parents use a special pouch in their mouth for carrying food to their young.

5 The baby bird's adult feathers have started to grow. It calls to its parents to bring it food.

The nestling still has fluffy gray down on its back and neck.

6 The young bird is not as colorful as its parents, but it has adult feathers and can fly.

7 The bird is now nine months old and is fully grown. The bullfinch is a shy bird, but its bright colors make it easy to spot when it does appear in fields and backyards.

Nesting material

The nest is a flimsy platform of twigs and roots hidden among the leaves of a tree or bush. The female bullfinch builds the nest by herself, and can be seen collecting nesting material in spring.

Common Starling

Common starlings are very adaptable birds, and they live in many parts of the world. They are found in both cities and the countryside. The female lays a clutch of four to six eggs, usually once a year. She lays one egg every day, often in the morning. The female does most of the incubating, but the male sits on the eggs for a few hours each day. They are ready to hatch after 12 days.

1 Common starling eggs range in color from white to pale blue. The egg starts to hatch after it has been incubated for two weeks.

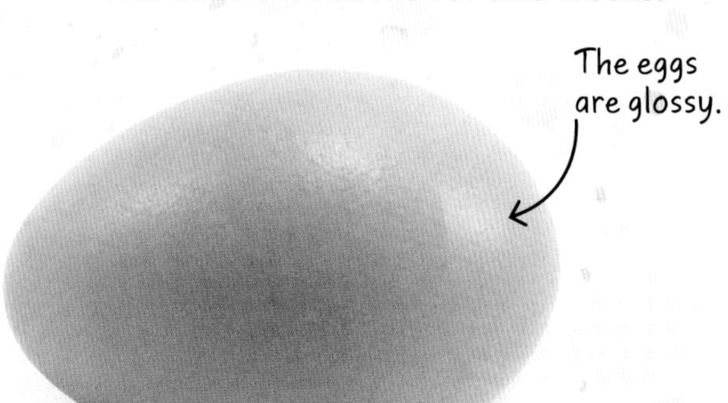

The eggs are glossy.

2 The chick works its way around the egg to make a crack in the eggshell.

Holes at blunt end of egg

14 hours and 55 minutes later

Hollow nest

Common starlings build their nests in holes in trees and buildings. Each nest is a mass of twigs, leaves, and grass. These birds also lay their eggs in birdhouses.

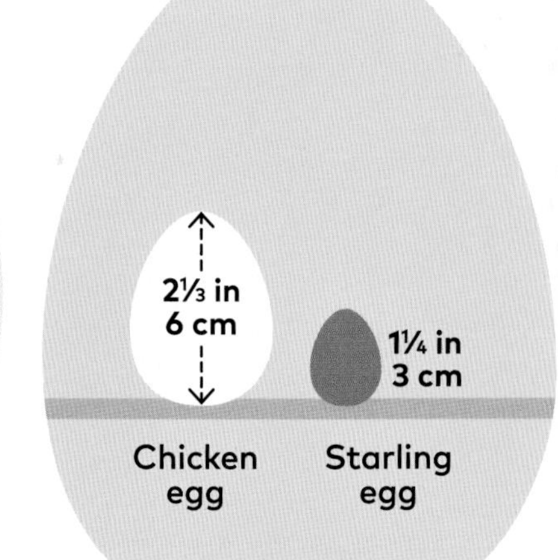

During fall and winter, the feathers have pale tips, which make the bird look spotted.
6
At nine months old, the starling is fully grown. Adult birds eat a lot of things, including worms, insects, and seeds. In summer, the starling's beak changes color from brown to yellow.
5
Young starlings leave the nest after around three weeks. Their parents continue to feed them for several days.
20 days later
5 minutes later
1 minute later
Down
3
As the chick starts to hatch out, its pink body can be seen. It pushes hard to widen the crack in the eggshell.
4
The whole end of the eggshell lifts away. The chick has some down, but its feathers are damp.

1 Swan eggs vary in color from pale brown to gray-green. The chick has made a small break in the eggshell.

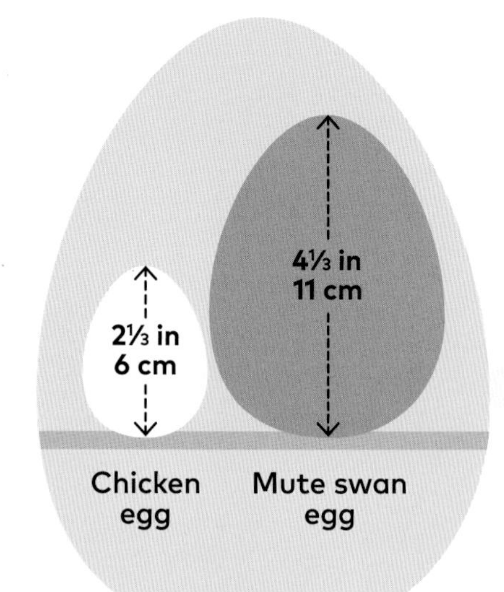

16 hours and 10 minutes later

2 The baby swan, called a cygnet, cuts off the blunt end of the eggshell by pecking it with its beak.

3 The cygnet gradually straightens its long neck and pushes its way out of the broken eggshell.

25 minutes later

Mute swans build a huge nest of plants, often on an island or on the bank of a river or pond. The nest measures up to 6 ft (2 m) across and 31 in (80 cm) high. The male picks plants, and then the female builds the nest and lines it with her soft down. The female lays four to eight eggs and sits on them for five weeks.

Taxi service

Very young birds, such as these cygnets, are at risk from both predators and the cold of the water. Their parents take turns carrying the chicks on their back to keep them safe, dry, and warm.

4 minutes later

4 The baby swan often rests while it is hatching. A white egg tooth can be seen on the tip of its beak. This was used to cut through the eggshell and will wear away altogether in a few days.

5 The cygnet is now two days old. It is already able to go swimming with its parents. The young bird's gray-brown down will turn white by the time it is one year old.

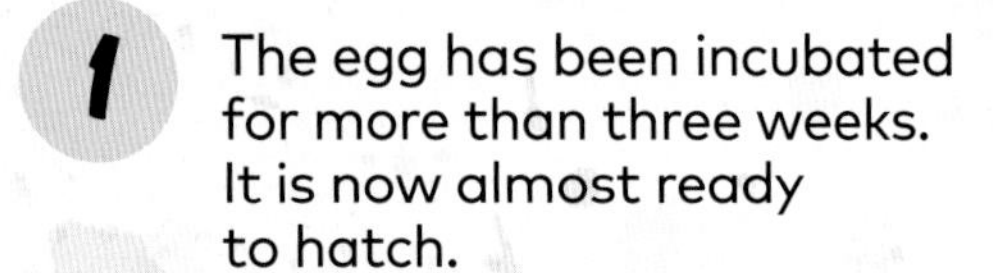

1 The egg has been incubated for more than three weeks. It is now almost ready to hatch.

2 Hatching has started. The first pieces of eggshell break off as the chick pecks at the shell from the inside.

27 minutes later

Crowned Lapwing

The crowned lapwing lives on the grassy plains of eastern and southern Africa. The female lays two or three eggs in a shallow dip in the ground. The eggs are pointed at one end, which allows them to lie close together in the nest and fit snugly under their parents. They are ready to hatch after 25 days of incubation.

Hidden eggs

The crowned lapwing surrounds its eggs with pebbles and dry grass. This keeps the eggs safe because they are hard to see. If a predator approaches, one parent moves away from the nest and screams to distract it.

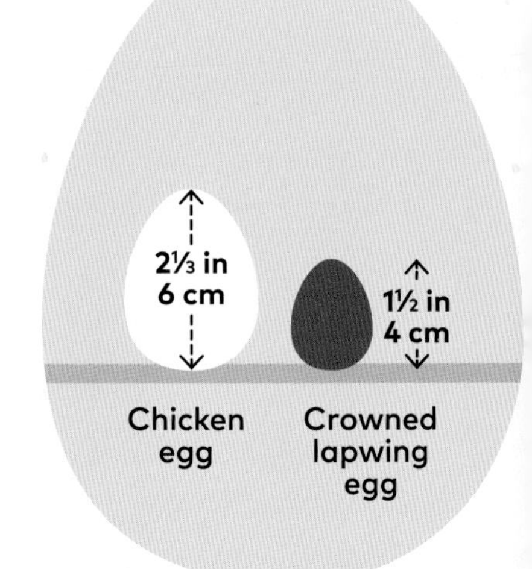

3 The chick has burst open the eggshell and is pushing itself out. Its head and wings emerge first.

4 The chick has straightened its neck and has thrust off the end of the eggshell. It is resting but will soon be able to sit up.

5 The chick is now two days old. Baby crowned lapwings soon leave the nest and run around with their parents, who show them where to find the right food. They can catch insects and other small animals by themselves.

Common pigeon

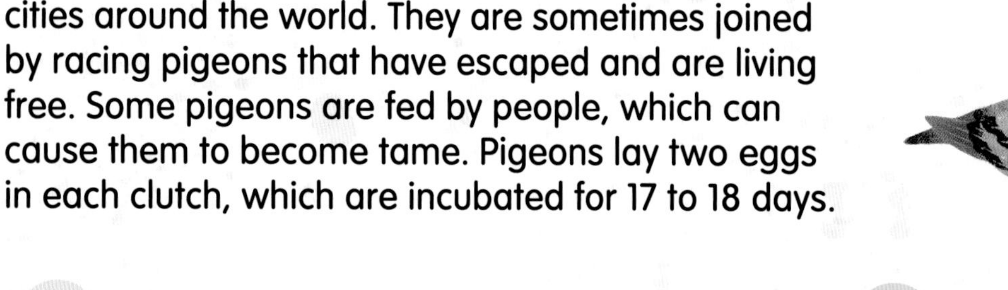

Common pigeons live in large flocks in towns and cities around the world. They are sometimes joined by racing pigeons that have escaped and are living free. Some pigeons are fed by people, which can cause them to become tame. Pigeons lay two eggs in each clutch, which are incubated for 17 to 18 days.

1 Common pigeon eggs are a glossy white color. This egg has now cracked, 17 hours after it was first pipped.

4 hours and 15 minutes later

2 The crack slowly grows over a few hours. A large crack shows that the chick will soon come out of the eggshell.

The baby pigeon can be seen through the crack.

15 minutes later

3 The crack now stretches all the way around the blunt end of the eggshell. The top of the eggshell is pushed off by the chick inside.

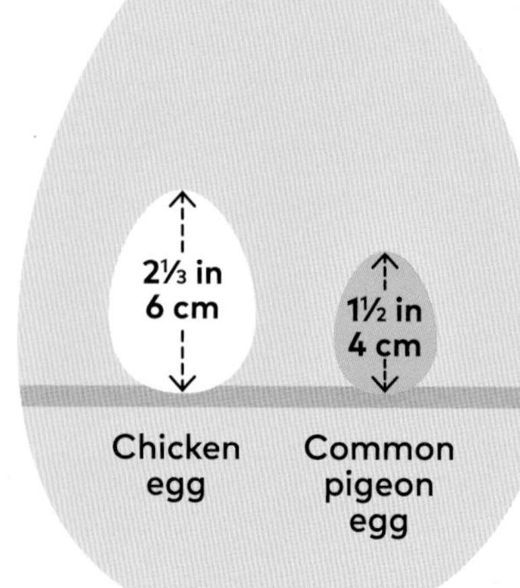

Unusual nest

A pigeon's nest of twigs is usually built on a ledge or in a hole in a building, wherever it can find space. Like their wild relatives, common pigeons build their nests high up to keep their chicks safe from predators.

1 hour and 55 minutes later

4 The baby pigeon, called a squab, is finally free. It is already dry and fluffy. It will be fed for the first 10 days on a liquid, known as "milk," made in its parents' throats.

5 The young pigeon is now two weeks old. It is called a squeaker because it squeaks when it wants to be fed. It will be able to fly when it is 35 days old.

Tawny owl

Most tawny owls live in forests, but some live in towns or open country with few trees. These birds pair up for life and live together all year round. The female usually lays two or three eggs. She starts to incubate them as soon as the first egg is laid. The eggs hatch after four weeks over a number of days, in the order they were laid.

1 This egg was pipped more than 24 hours ago. The chick waits in the egg until the remains of the yolk are absorbed into its body.

2 The chick presses its beak in the same spot until small pieces of eggshell fall off and a hole is made.

3 The chick works fast to chip out a series of holes with its egg tooth. The holes are so close together that they make a slit. When the slit opens up, the end of the egg lifts away.

4 As the chick pushes, the slit widens until a wing escapes from the eggshell. The chick's neck is still curled around, but it tries to straighten it.

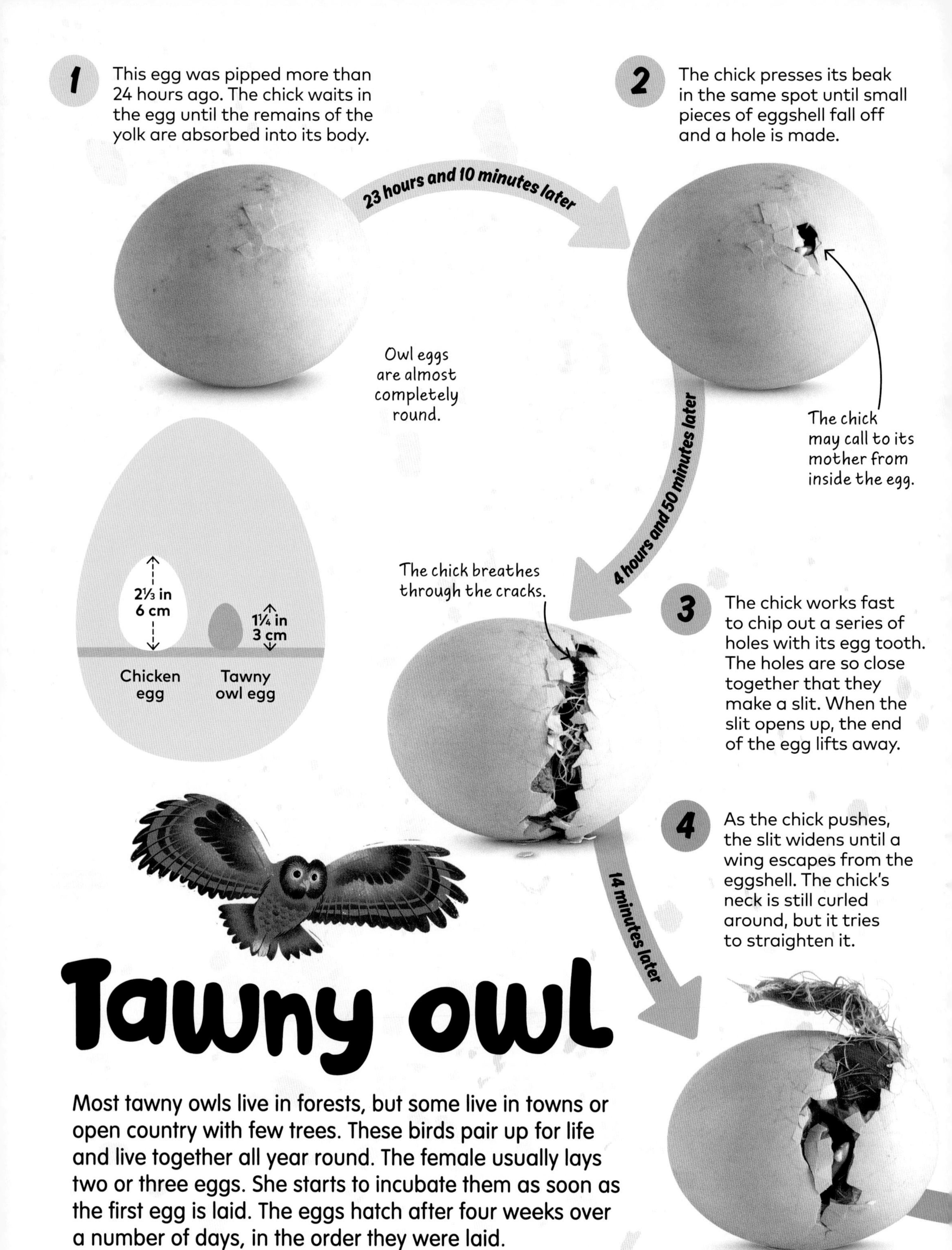

7 At 12 weeks old, the owlet can fly and is learning to hunt for itself. However, it still relies on its parents to bring it food. It can swallow a mouse whole!

The tawny owl only comes out at night but its well-known hooting often reveals where it is.

6 The owlet is now two days old. It keeps its eyes shut for most of the time until it is around two weeks old. It twitters when it is hungry.

The chick is finally free after more than 55 hours.

5 The mother owl will continue to stay with the newly hatched owlet. The warmth of her body will soon dry its down. The owlet does not feed on the first day.

Borrowed home

The female tawny owl does not build a nest. Instead, she uses the abandoned nest of another bird, or finds a hole in a tree. Tawny owls also use birdhouses put up by people. Both parents feed the nestlings.

Miniature nest

The tiny Anna's hummingbird is found along the western coast of North America. Its small nest is made by the female alone. She uses down, spiders' webs, and lichen—which is added as an outer covering to provide camouflage.

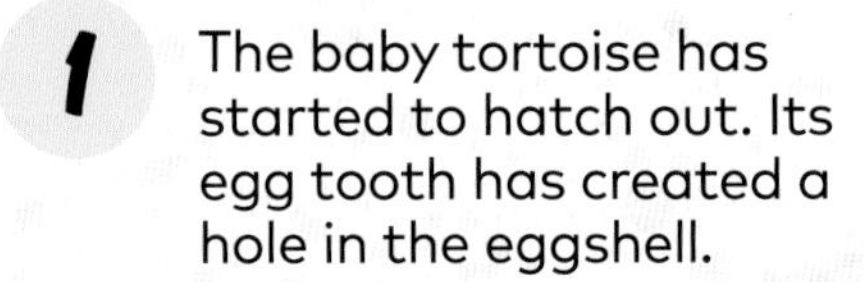

1 The baby tortoise has started to hatch out. Its egg tooth has created a hole in the eggshell.

2 The tortoise turns around inside its egg while it hatches, so it can break another part of the eggshell.

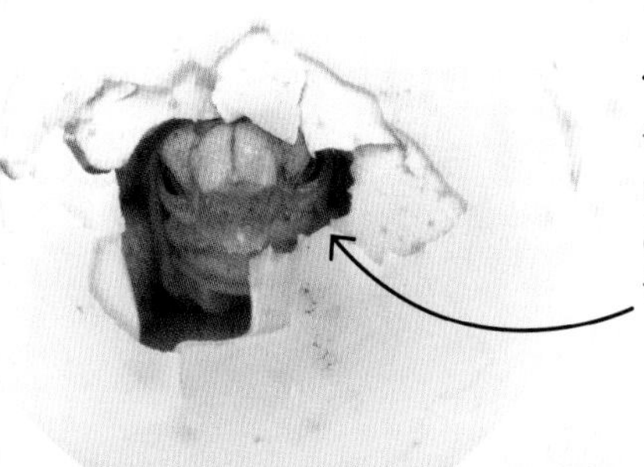

The baby tortoise is peeping out of the hole in the eggshell.

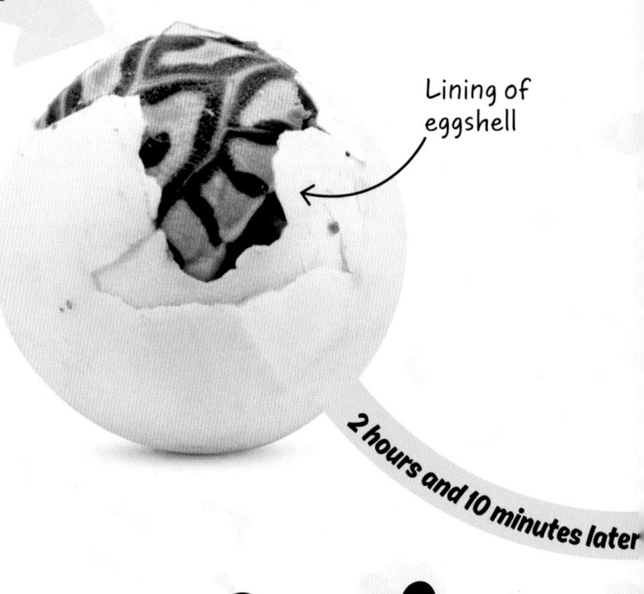

Leopard tortoise

All tortoises live in warm areas. The leopard tortoise is found in many countries in Africa south of the Sahara Desert. It eats grass and juicy plants, and adults can grow to more than 14 in (35 cm) long. Tortoise eggs can be hard or soft, but the leopard tortoise lays hard eggs. Females lay 10 to 25 eggs in each clutch.

Digging a hole

When the female is ready to lay her eggs, she digs a hole in the ground with her back feet, drops the eggs in, and covers them with soil. The eggs hatch more quickly in warm ground. If the soil stays at 86°F (30°C), they will hatch in around five months.

3 The young tortoise bites off pieces of the eggshell to make the hole larger.

4 By pushing hard with its front legs, the baby tortoise manages to break out of the egg.

The baby tortoise takes a good look around before it goes any further.

5 The hole is now so big that the baby tortoise can walk out of its eggshell.

The baby tortoise's shell is still soft and folded underneath, but it will soon unfold and harden.

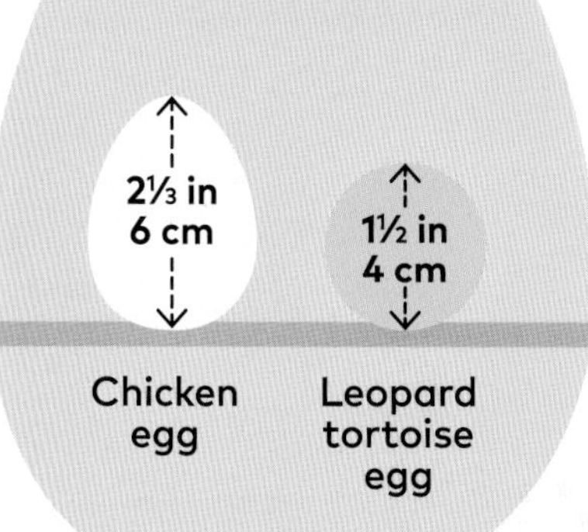

6 The young tortoise crawls away from the nest and soon starts to eat. From a young age, it eats the same grasses and leaves as its parents. The spots on the tortoise's shell are clearly visible, and are what give the leopard tortoise its name.

Corn Snake

The corn snake lives in North America. This colorful reptile is often kept as a pet. Its name comes from its habit of living in cornfields. Corn snakes often climb trees and eat bird eggs and nestlings. The female lays around 8 to 16 soft eggs, which hatch after six to eight weeks.

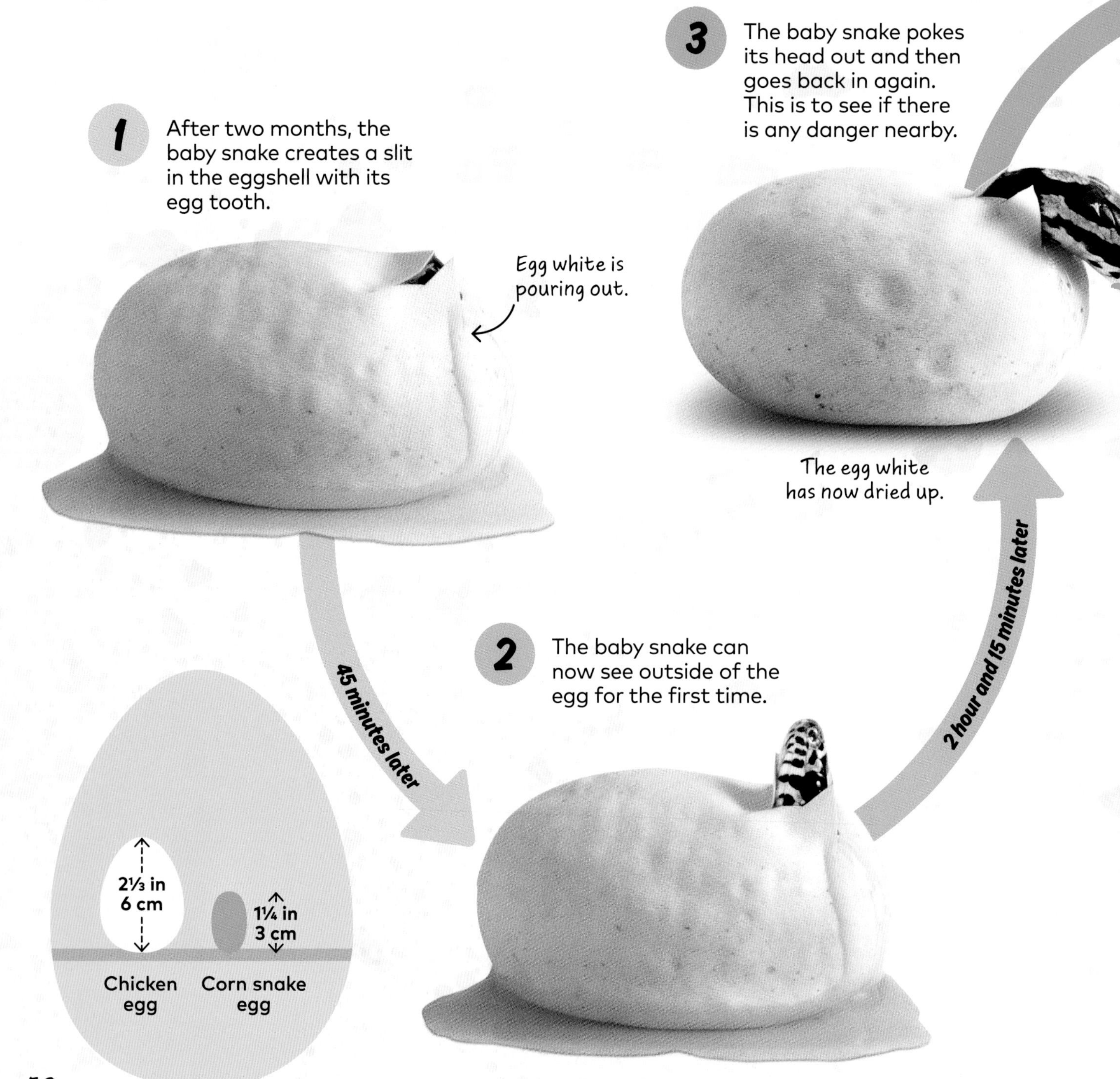

Plant nest

Female corn snakes often lay their eggs in rotting plants or a tree stump. Once laid, the mother snake doesn't look after her clutch. The rotting plants release heat as they break down, which helps to keep the eggs warm.

21 hours and 30 minutes later

4 When it is safe to do so, the snake hatchling suddenly slithers out of the egg and glides away.

One day after first piercing the eggshell, the baby snake emerges from a second hole.

The young snake checks its surroundings by tasting the air with its tongue.

5 The snake is newly hatched. It will shed its skin when it is a few days old. The young corn snake never sees its parents. It lives on the yolk sac within its body for a few days before starting to hunt for prey, such as frogs and lizards.

Leopard gecko

The leopard gecko is a kind of lizard. It lives in the grasslands of India, Pakistan, and Iran. It makes its nest in a hole in the ground, in which it lays two soft, white eggs. Geckos come out to hunt at night. The leopard gecko feeds on insects. It stalks its prey and then pounces, just like a cat hunting a mouse.

1 Sand and dirt stuck to the egg make it look speckled. The eggshell has just split open.

Split in eggshell

2 The gecko forces the split wider by pushing against it with its head. Soon it will be able to fit its head through.

5 minutes later

New skin

Young geckos shed, or molt, their scaly skin often to allow them to grow rapidly. As adults, they molt around once a month. Geckos sometimes eat their old skin to recover the nutrients it still contains.

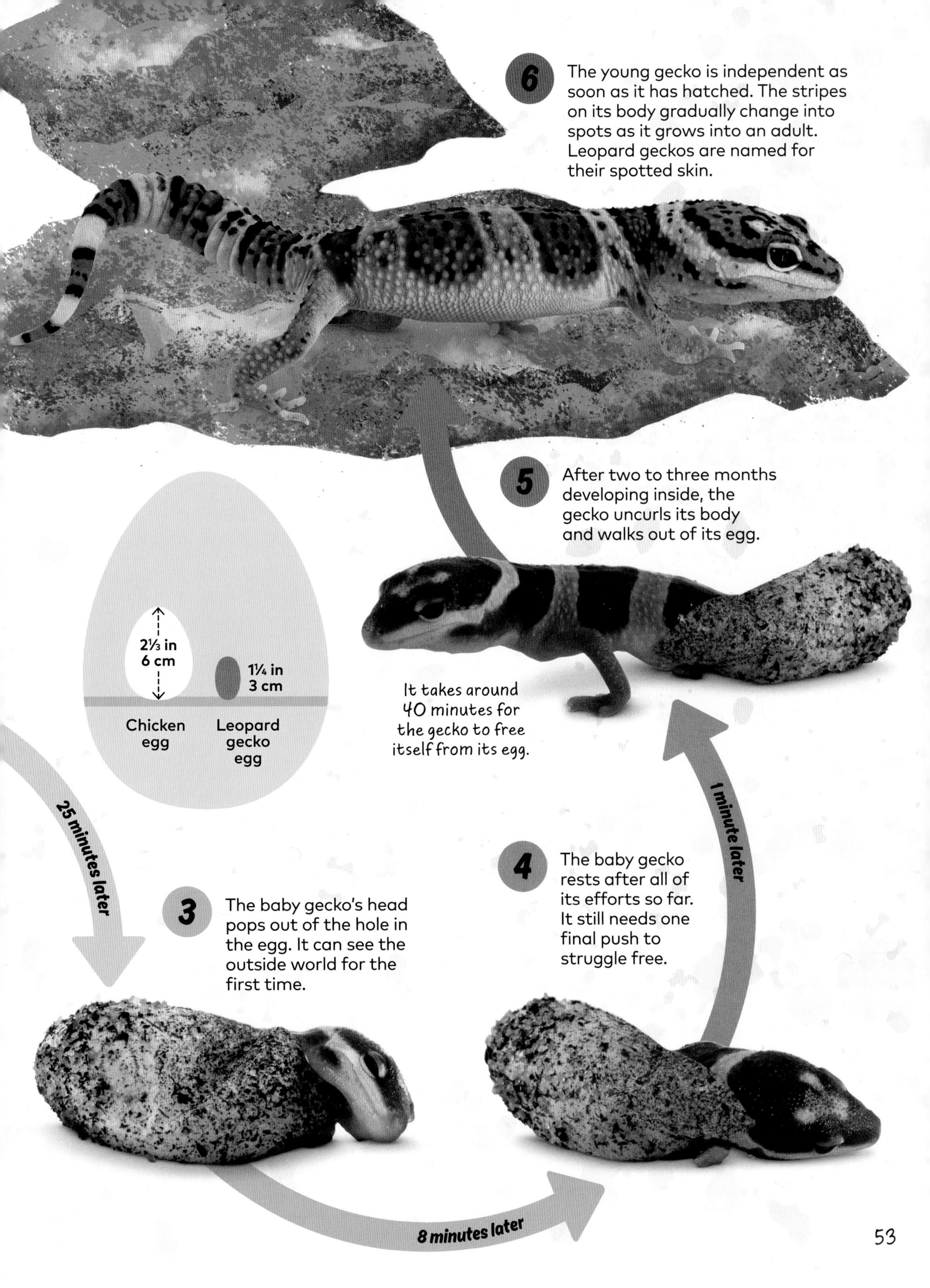
6
The young gecko is independent as soon as it has hatched. The stripes on its body gradually change into spots as it grows into an adult. Leopard geckos are named for their spotted skin.
5
After two to three months developing inside, the gecko uncurls its body and walks out of its egg.
2⅓ in
6 cm
1¼ in
3 cm
Chicken egg
Leopard gecko egg
It takes around 40 minutes for the gecko to free itself from its egg.
1 minute later
25 minutes later
4
The baby gecko rests after all of its efforts so far. It still needs one final push to struggle free.
3
The baby gecko's head pops out of the hole in the egg. It can see the outside world for the first time.
8 minutes later

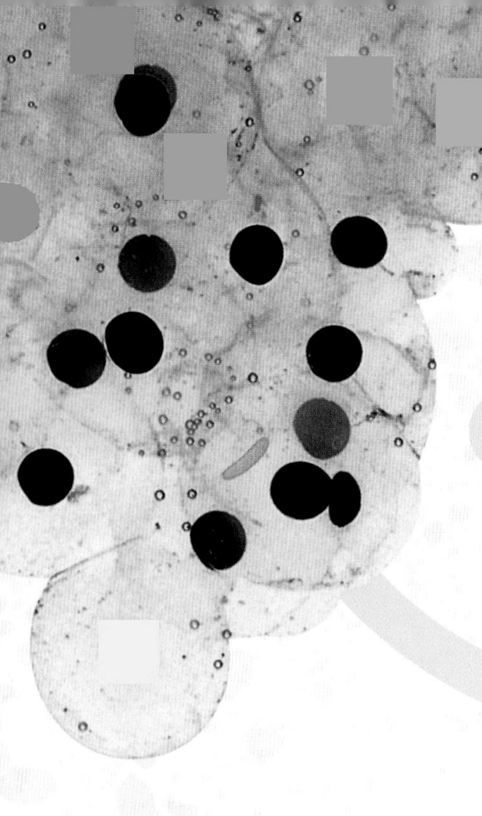

The eggs have just been laid.

1 A frog egg looks like a black dot surrounded by a ball of transparent, or see-through, jelly.

9 days later

2 A tadpole has formed at the center of the egg and is almost ready to hatch out.

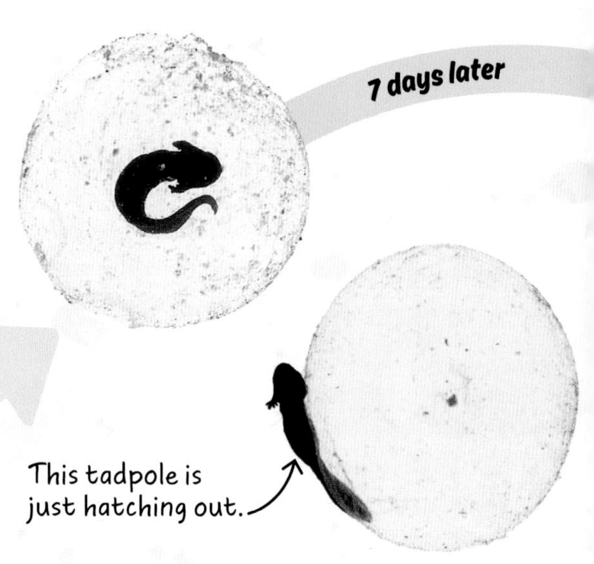

7 days later

This tadpole is just hatching out.

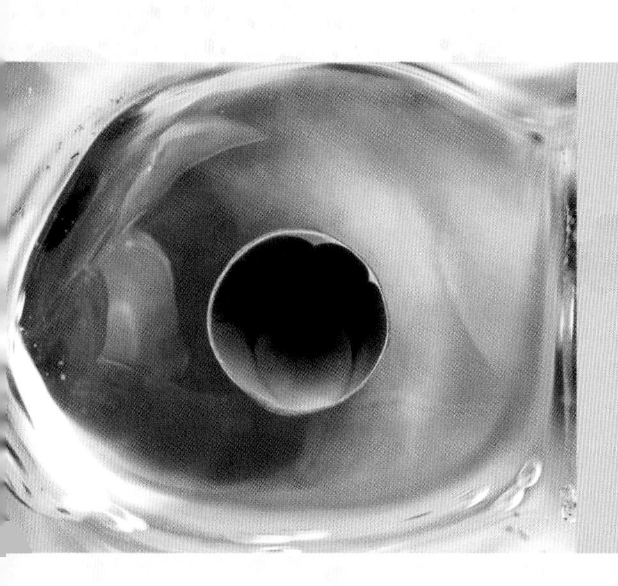

See-through eggshell

Frogs produce many eggs that stick together in the water. These clumps of jelly-coated eggs are known as frogspawn. The eggs are see-through, so you can see the cell inside dividing and developing into a tadpole.

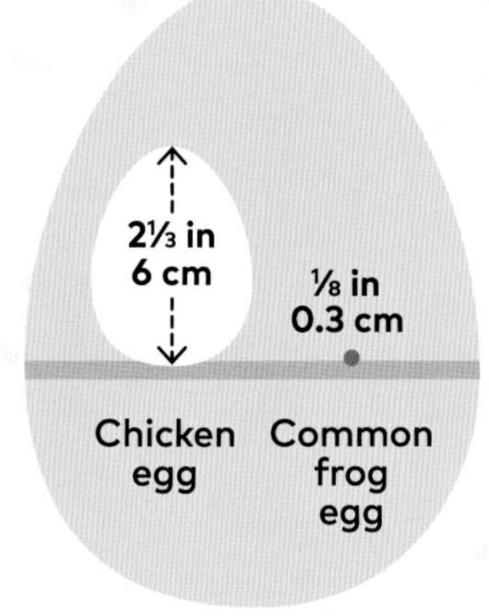

Common frog

Frogs are amphibians. These are animals that begin their lives in water, then move onto land. Adult common frogs spend most of their time on land, but every spring females find a pond and lay up to 1,000 eggs in the water. The eggs hatch into larvae, known as tadpoles, which live in the water until they grow into froglets.

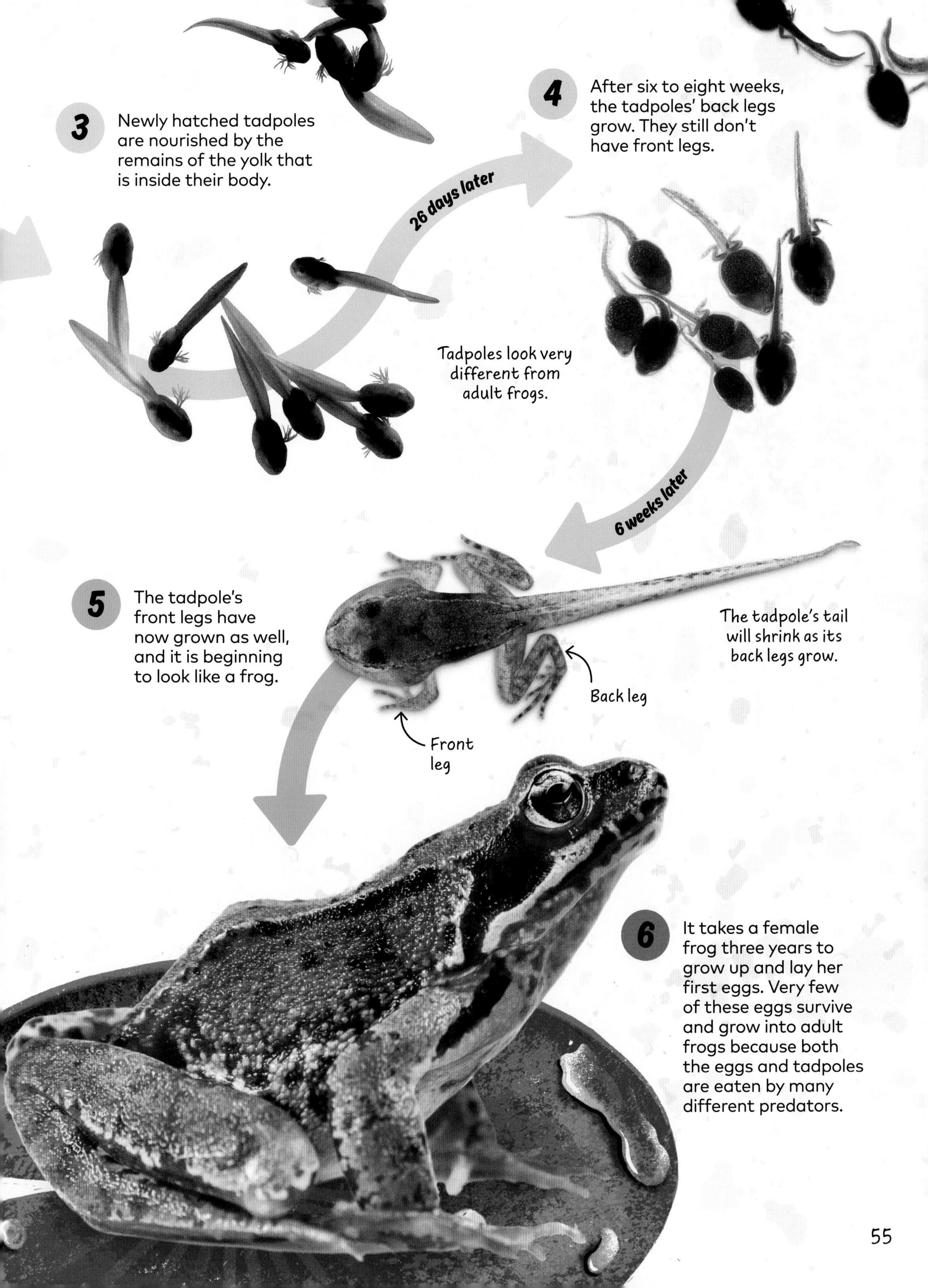
3
Newly hatched tadpoles are nourished by the remains of the yolk that is inside their body.
26 days later
4
After six to eight weeks, the tadpoles' back legs grow. They still don't have front legs.
Tadpoles look very different from adult frogs.
6 weeks later
5
The tadpole's front legs have now grown as well, and it is beginning to look like a frog.
The tadpole's tail will shrink as its back legs grow.
Back leg
Front leg
6
It takes a female frog three years to grow up and lay her first eggs. Very few of these eggs survive and grow into adult frogs because both the eggs and tadpoles are eaten by many different predators.

Great crested newt

Newts belong to a group of amphibians called salamanders. The adults always look like tadpoles because their tail doesn't disappear and their legs are small in comparison to their body. They live in damp places on land for much of their lives. Unlike frogs, newts stay in the water for several weeks after they have laid their eggs.

1 The newly laid egg is enclosed in jelly. This helps to protect the egg from animals that might eat it.

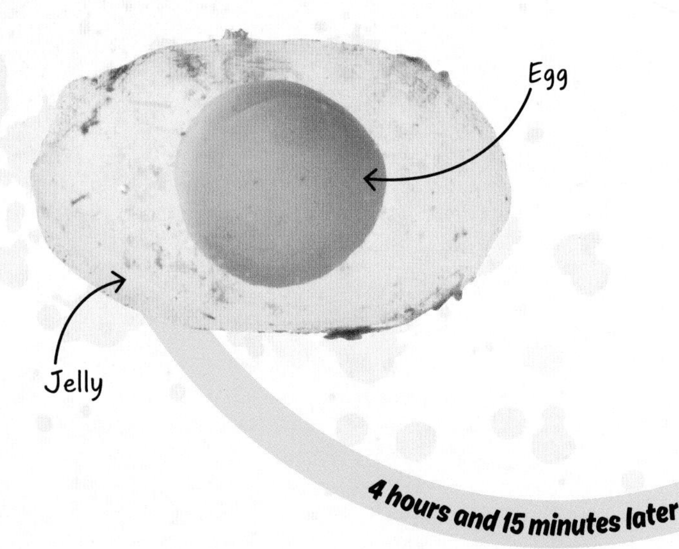

4 hours and 15 minutes later

2 The egg has divided into two cells. It will continue to divide, doubling the number of cells each time.

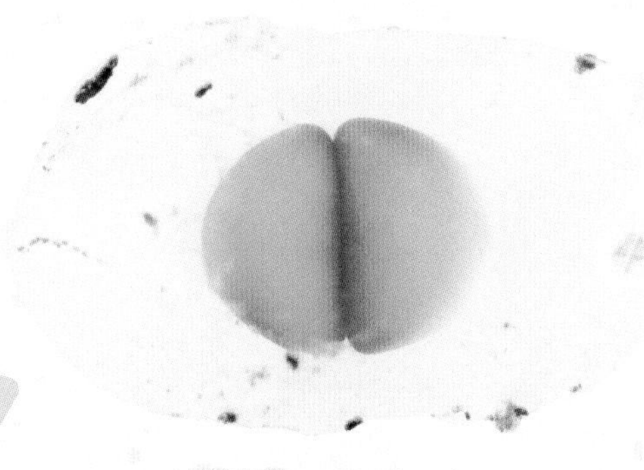

The cells divide very rapidly.

Leafy nest

During the spring and summer, the female newt lays 200 to 300 eggs. She wraps each egg in the leaf of a water plant. This hides the eggs from hungry predators.

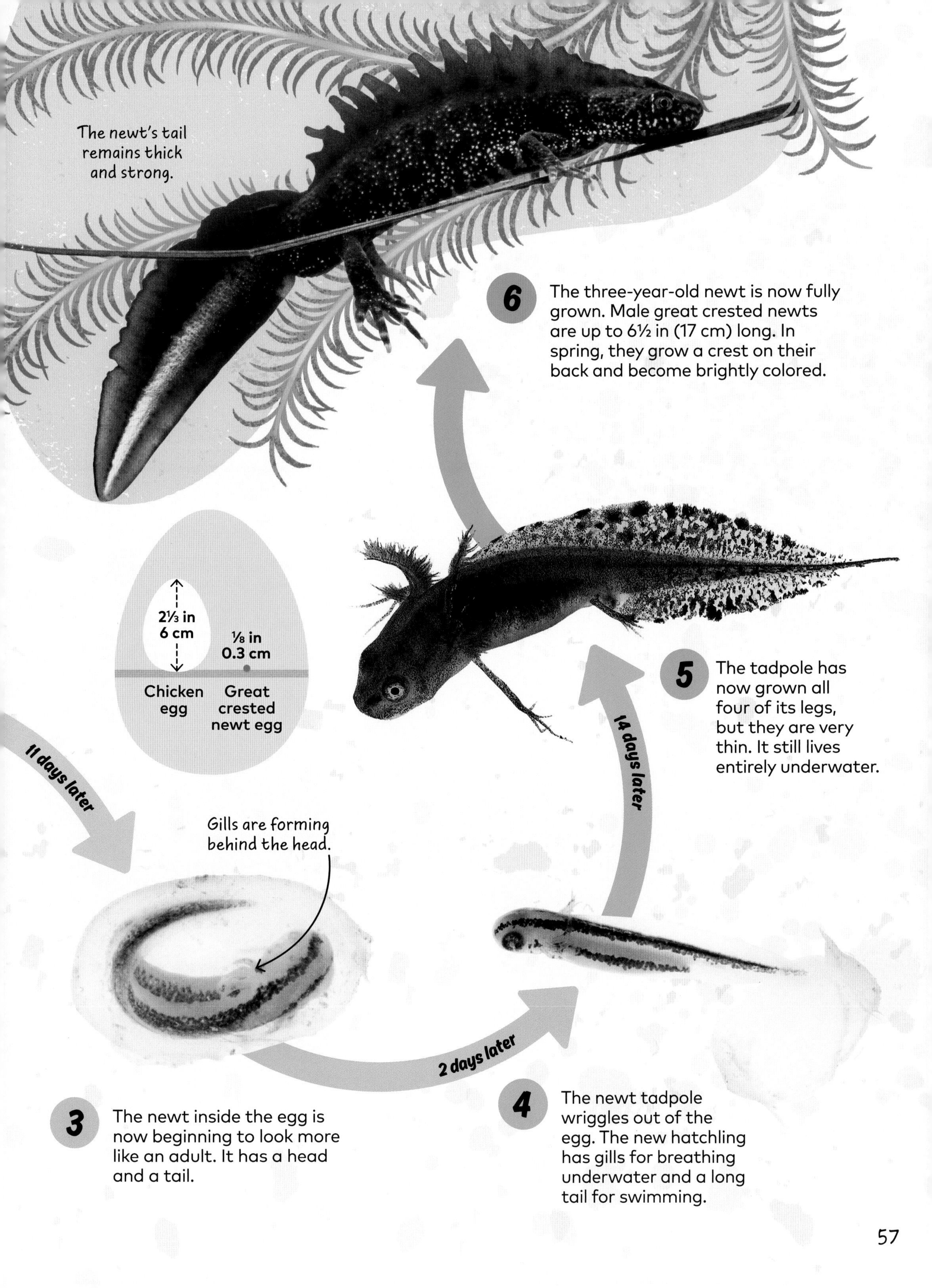

6 The three-year-old newt is now fully grown. Male great crested newts are up to 6½ in (17 cm) long. In spring, they grow a crest on their back and become brightly colored.

5 The tadpole has now grown all four of its legs, but they are very thin. It still lives entirely underwater.

3 The newt inside the egg is now beginning to look more like an adult. It has a head and a tail.

4 The newt tadpole wriggles out of the egg. The new hatchling has gills for breathing underwater and a long tail for swimming.

Eggs in strings

Common toads lay their eggs in long strands that look like necklaces. Each string contains two or three rows of eggs and is wrapped securely around water plants. The tadpoles hatch out after around 10 days.

Rainbow trout

This fish was originally found in the streams and rivers by the coasts of western North America and eastern Asia. It has also been introduced to many countries for food and fishing. Before the female lays her eggs, she scrapes out a nest in the gravel of a riverbed. Once the eggs have been fertilized by a male, she hides them under more gravel.

1 Two weeks after the egg is laid, the fish's body starts to take shape. Its eyes look like black dots.

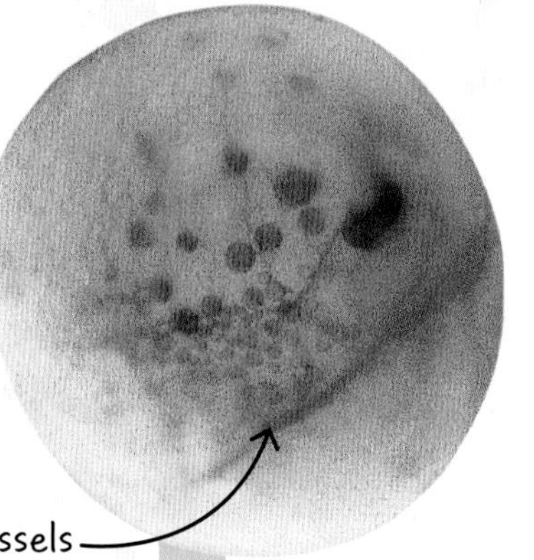

Blood vessels have already developed.

11 days later

2 The baby trout is wrapped around the yellow yolk. It is almost ready to wriggle out of the egg.

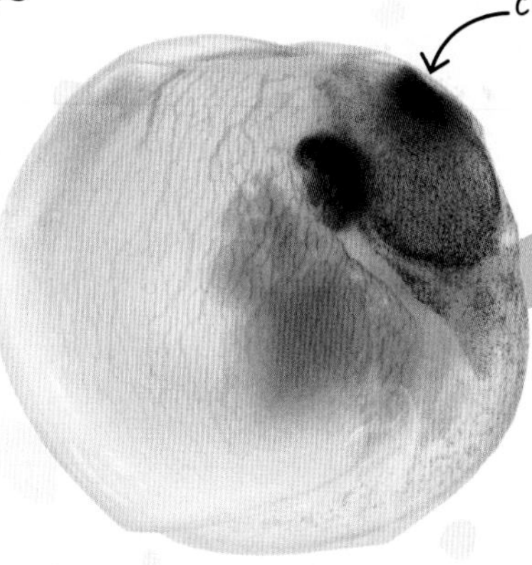

Each eye is clearly visible.

3 days later

3 The fish has broken through the soft egg case. It will hatch sooner in warmer waters.

The fish is emerging quickly.

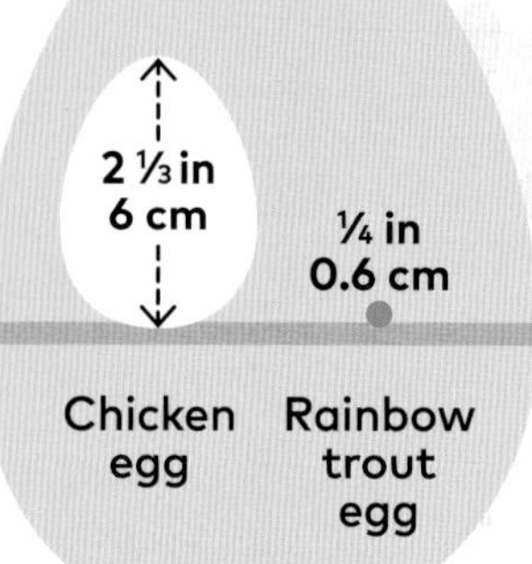

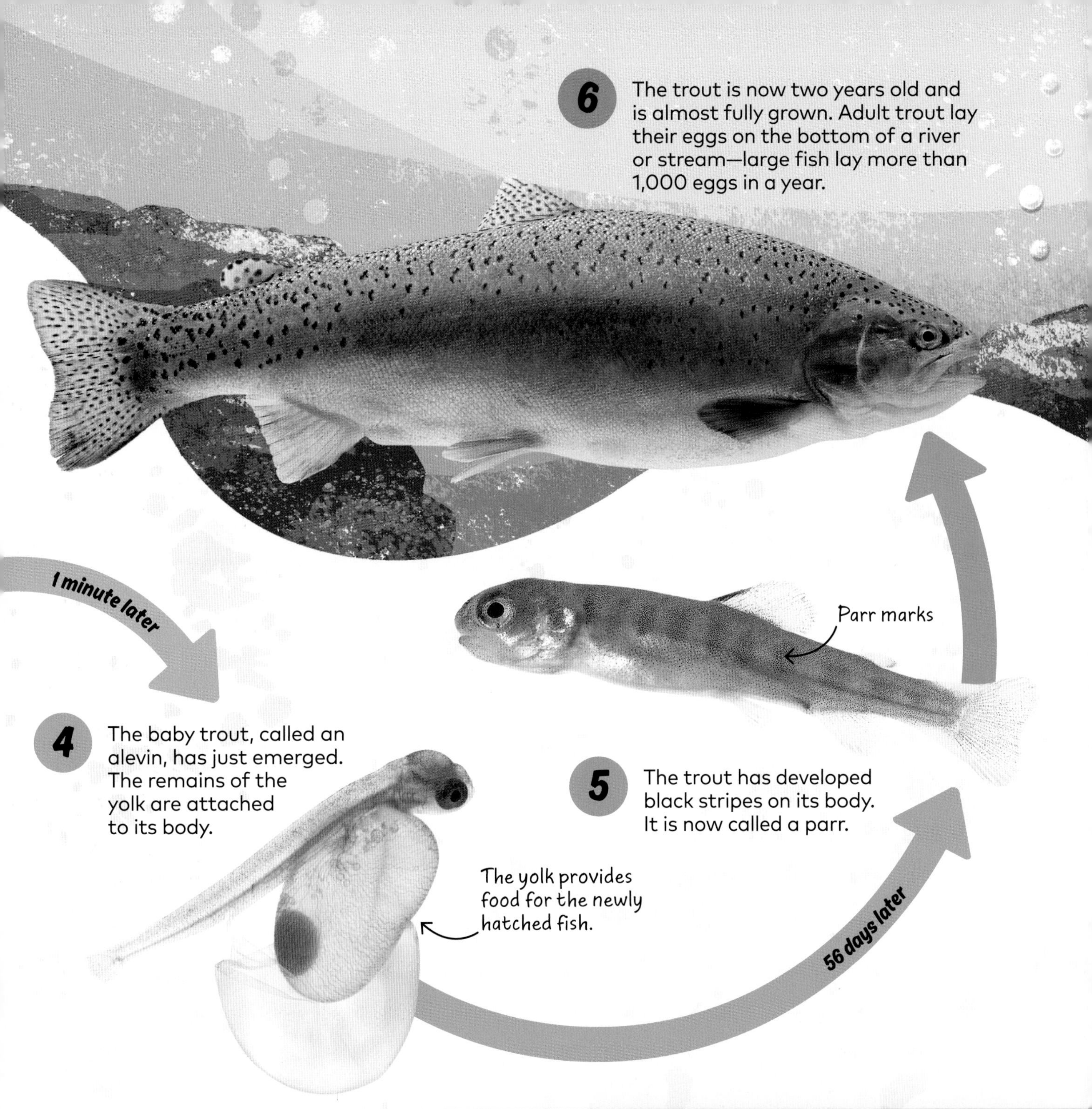

Breeding colors

The rainbow trout is named for the colorful stripe running along its side. The pink color brightens around the time that rainbow trout lay their eggs. These fish probably choose mates with brighter stripes.

1 Two days after the egg is laid, the fish has started to develop. It has a long body, and large black dots show where its eyes will be.

2 The baby goldfish curled up inside the eggs are now almost fully formed. They will soon hatch out.

4 days later

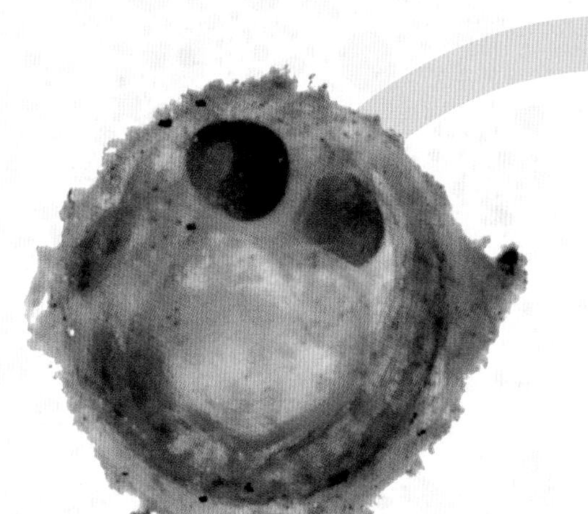

Goldfish eggs are round.

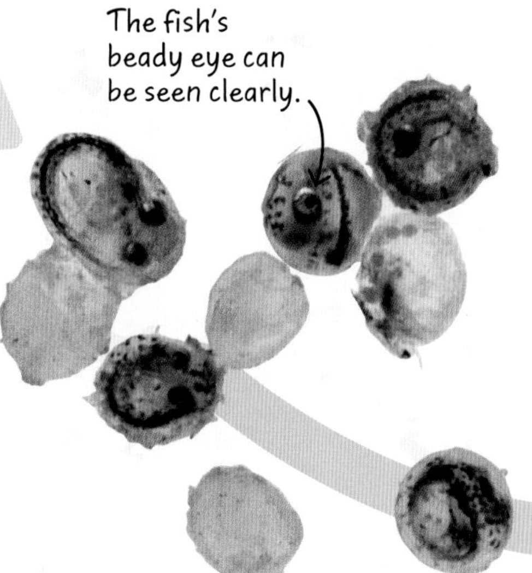

The fish's beady eye can be seen clearly.

Goldfish

Chicken egg	Goldfish egg
$2\frac{1}{3}$ in 6 cm	$\frac{1}{12}$ in 0.2 cm

Goldfish are often kept as pets in fish tanks. These bright little creatures belong to a group of fish called carp, but they look very different from their wild relatives. They were bred by humans for many years to create today's golden fish. Female goldfish scatter hundreds of eggs in the water at a time. The eggs are sticky and attach to water plants.

Colorful carp

The goldfish's wild carp ancestors were all a gray-green color. However, goldfish come in a variety of shades, including white, yellow, orange, red, and gold. Many also have black patches.

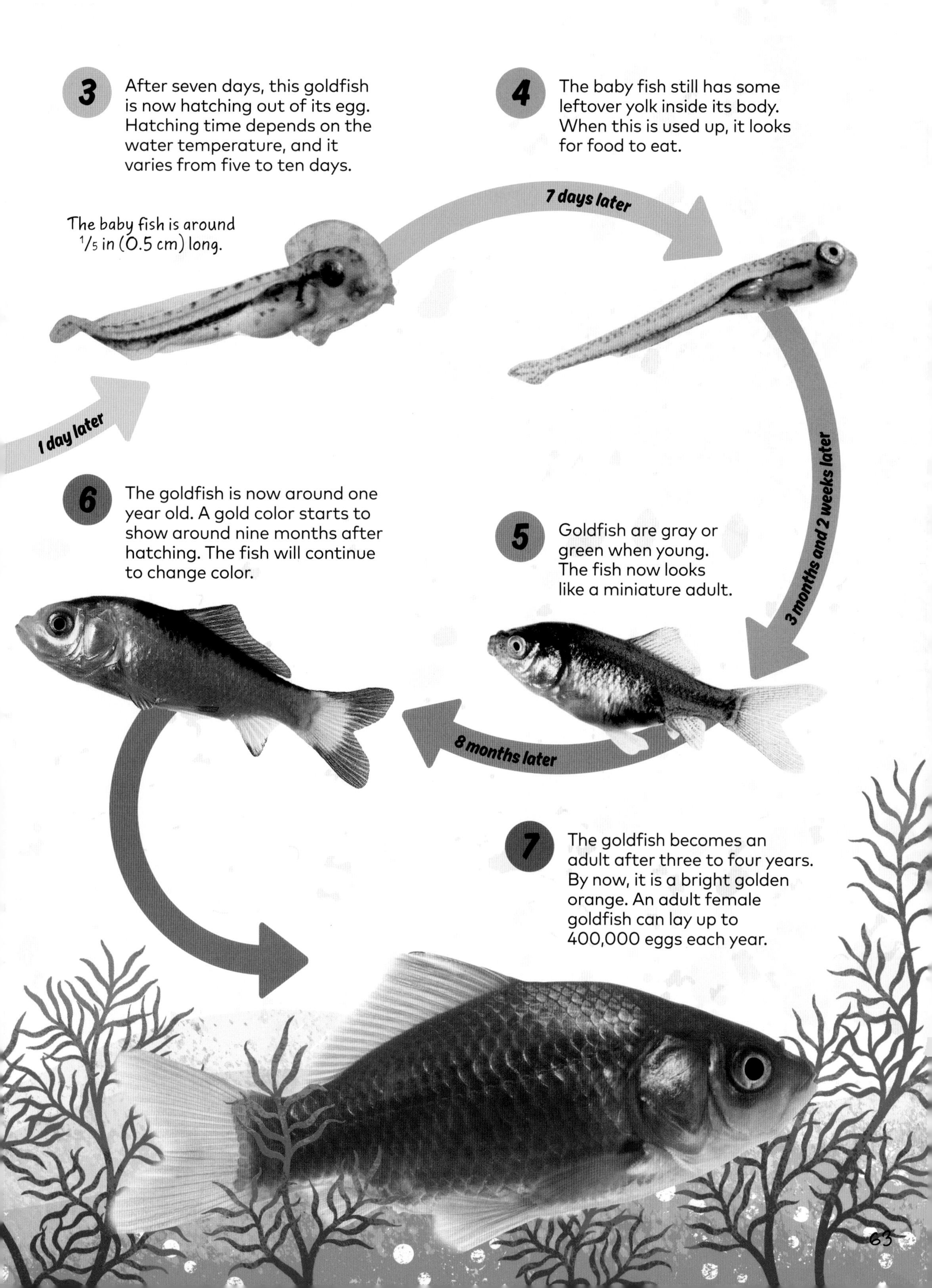

3
After seven days, this goldfish is now hatching out of its egg. Hatching time depends on the water temperature, and it varies from five to ten days.
4
The baby fish still has some leftover yolk inside its body. When this is used up, it looks for food to eat.
The baby fish is around 1/5 in (0.5 cm) long.
7 days later
1 day later
6
The goldfish is now around one year old. A gold color starts to show around nine months after hatching. The fish will continue to change color.
3 months and 2 weeks later
5
Goldfish are gray or green when young. The fish now looks like a miniature adult.
8 months later
7
The goldfish becomes an adult after three to four years. By now, it is a bright golden orange. An adult female goldfish can lay up to 400,000 eggs each year.

1 The egg is one of a clutch of around 20. Inside the egg, the baby dogfish has been growing for seven months.

2 Eight months after the egg was laid, the dogfish is ready to hatch out. It breaks open one end of its egg case.

The baby pokes its nose out of the egg case.

The baby dogfish is visible through the leathery case.

Mermaid's purse

Empty dogfish egg cases are called "mermaid's purses." They are often found on the beach. The curly tendrils at each end of the case were used to secure it to seaweed while the baby developed inside.

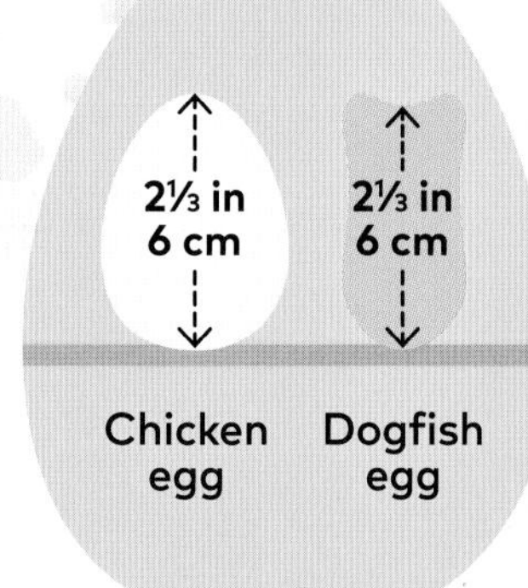

Dogfish

The lesser-spotted dogfish, or simply the dogfish, is a small shark found off the coasts of Europe and northern Africa. Like other sharks, dogfish lay smaller clutches of eggs than other fish. Their young are also much larger. Each egg is protected by a tough case, which is hidden among seaweed near the shore.

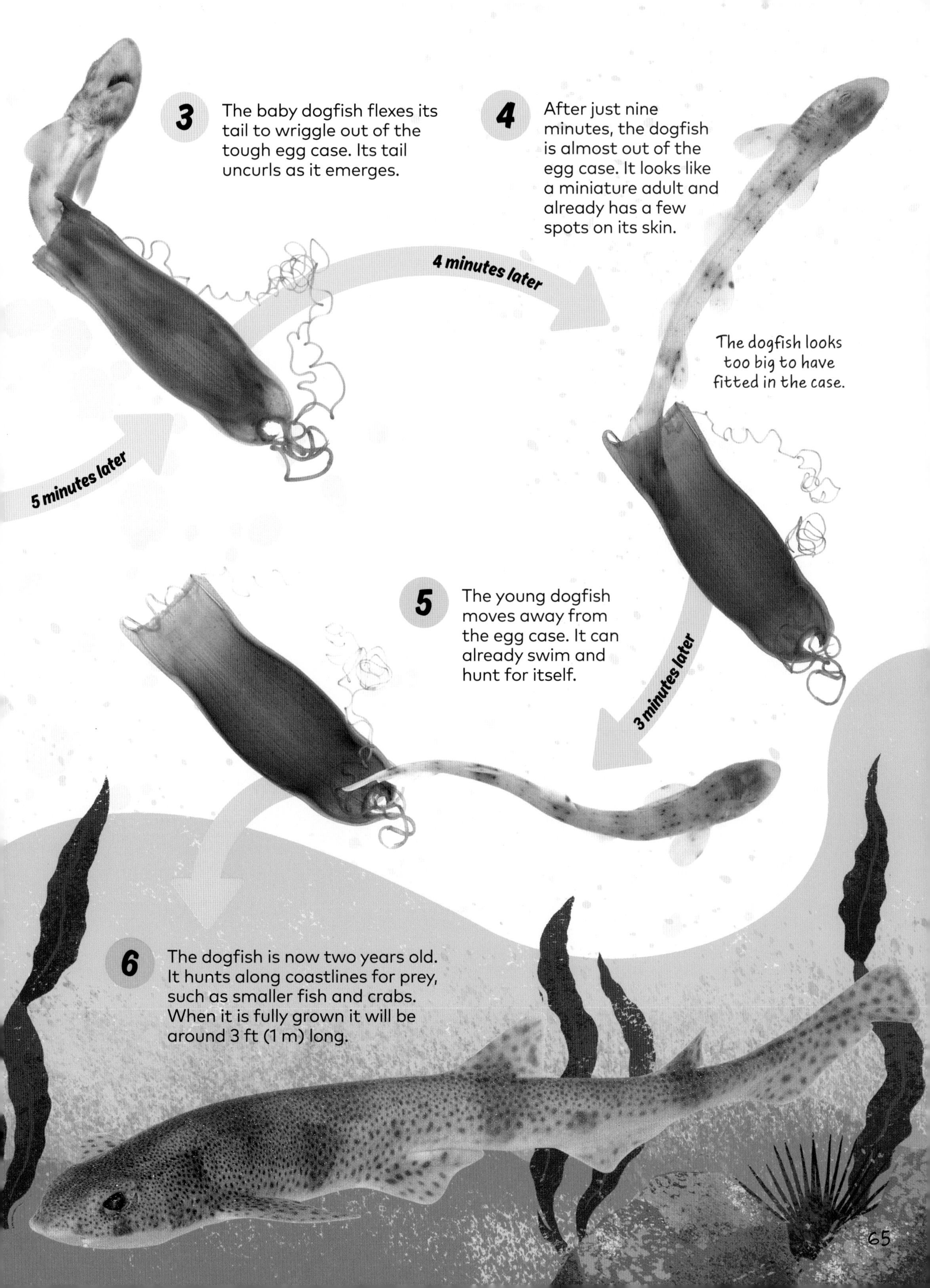
3
The baby dogfish flexes its tail to wriggle out of the tough egg case. Its tail uncurls as it emerges.
4 minutes later
4
After just nine minutes, the dogfish is almost out of the egg case. It looks like a miniature adult and already has a few spots on its skin.
The dogfish looks too big to have fitted in the case.
5 minutes later
5
The young dogfish moves away from the egg case. It can already swim and hunt for itself.
3 minutes later
6
The dogfish is now two years old. It hunts along coastlines for prey, such as smaller fish and crabs. When it is fully grown it will be around 3 ft (1 m) long.

Swell shark

This shark lives on the eastern coasts of the Pacific Ocean. It lays two flat eggs at a time. They are leathery with long ridges on them.

Spotted ratfish

Like sharks, ratfish lay eggs with tough cases. These stay attached to the female for a few days after being laid. The eggs hatch after a year.

Horn shark

Horn sharks produce spiral-edged eggs. The female may pick them up and wedge them in a rock crevice to secure them in place.

Fish eggs

Most kinds of fish lay a lot of small, soft-shelled eggs. They do this because their eggs are a favorite food of all sorts of aquatic animals and many are eaten. Sharks and their relatives, such as rays, lay fewer eggs, which are larger and have a leathery case to protect them. Some fish don't lay eggs at all, but give birth to babies.

Undulate ray

Female undulate rays lay up to 30 eggs every year. Each baby ray uncurls its side fins like scrolls of paper as it hatches from its case.

Sockeye salmon

Salmon live in the ocean, but they return to the freshwater rivers where they hatched to lay their own eggs. The salmon swim upstream to get there.

Northern pike

These fish are predators of other fish. They live in freshwater and lay a lot of sticky, yellow eggs that attach to water plants.

Common blenny

Common blennies are small fish, often found in rock pools. Males guard their colorful eggs closely until they are ready to hatch.

Grayling

Grayling live in freshwater and have a long back fin. They dig shallow dips, called redds, in gravelly riverbeds. Here, they lay their eggs.

Armored catfish

These South American fish have plates of bone under their skin to protect their body. The male guards the eggs from predators.

Brook lamprey

Brook lampreys lay their eggs in streambeds. Once the young hatch, they stay hidden in the mud for three to seven years before transforming into adults.

Underneath a Leaf

Female swallowtails are ready to mate and lay eggs as soon as they have emerged from their chrysalises. They normally lay one egg at a time on a plant, such as fennel, that the caterpillars will eat.

Swallowtail butterfly

This large butterfly is found across Asia, Europe, and North America. Adult butterflies look very different from their young. After the larvae, called caterpillars, have emerged from their eggs and grown in size, they transform into butterflies in a process called metamorphosis. The swallowtail lives for only a short time, during which it must mate and lay its eggs.

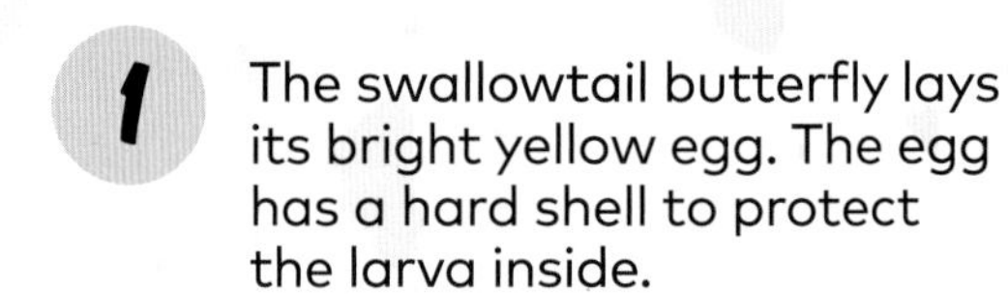

1 The swallowtail butterfly lays its bright yellow egg. The egg has a hard shell to protect the larva inside.

The egg will change from yellow to brown as the larva grows inside.

9 days later

2 The caterpillar doesn't have an egg tooth like a bird. Instead, it uses its jaws to cut a hole in the eggshell.

The caterpillar is starting to emerge.

2 hours later

3 As the caterpillar comes out of the egg, its body swells. It will eat the rest of the eggshell, which is full of nutrients.

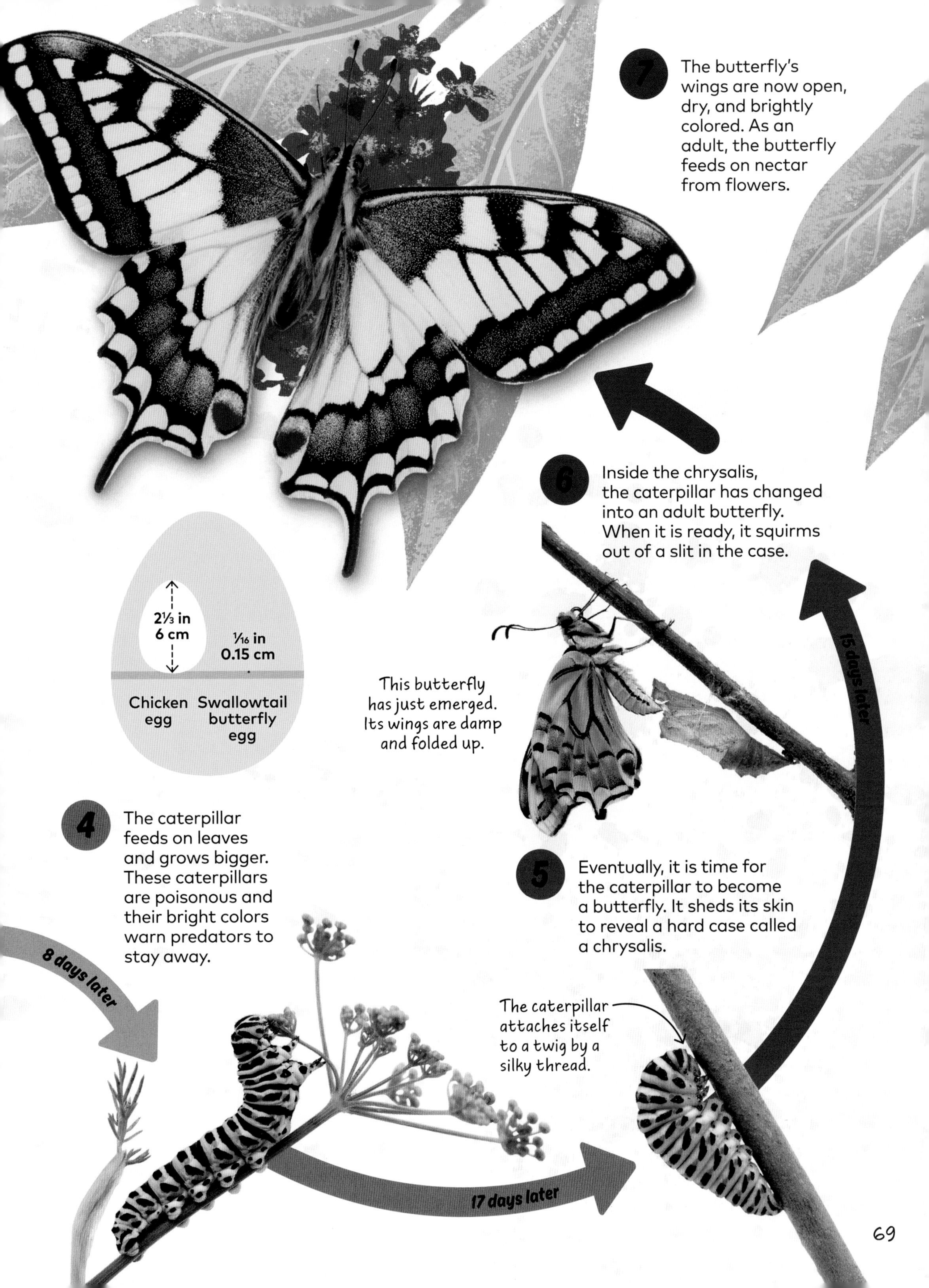
7
The butterfly's wings are now open, dry, and brightly colored. As an adult, the butterfly feeds on nectar from flowers.
6
Inside the chrysalis, the caterpillar has changed into an adult butterfly. When it is ready, it squirms out of a slit in the case.
15 days later
2⅓ in
6 cm
1⁄16 in
0.15 cm
Chicken egg
Swallowtail butterfly egg
This butterfly has just emerged. Its wings are damp and folded up.
4
The caterpillar feeds on leaves and grows bigger. These caterpillars are poisonous and their bright colors warn predators to stay away.
5
Eventually, it is time for the caterpillar to become a butterfly. It sheds its skin to reveal a hard case called a chrysalis.
8 days later
The caterpillar attaches itself to a twig by a silky thread.
17 days later

Seven-spotted Ladybug

The seven-spotted ladybug is found in many countries across the world, in parks, gardens, forests, and fields. This bright beetle is easily recognizable from the seven black spots on its shiny, red wing cases. It lays batches of around 15 to 20 eggs. These hatch into larvae, which go through metamorphosis to transform into adult ladybugs.

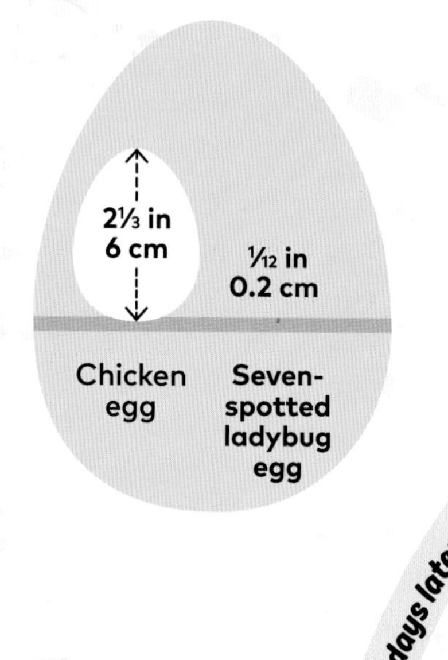

1 The ladybug lays a group of eggs, often under a leaf.

The eggs are bright yellow.

5 days later

2 The eggs turn brown just before they hatch.

1 day later

3 The eggs hatch together, and the larvae crawl away.

Aphid eater

As both an adult and a larva, the ladybug is a ferocious predator of tiny bugs called aphids. Because aphids are a pest that can damage plants, ladybugs are known as the gardener's friend.

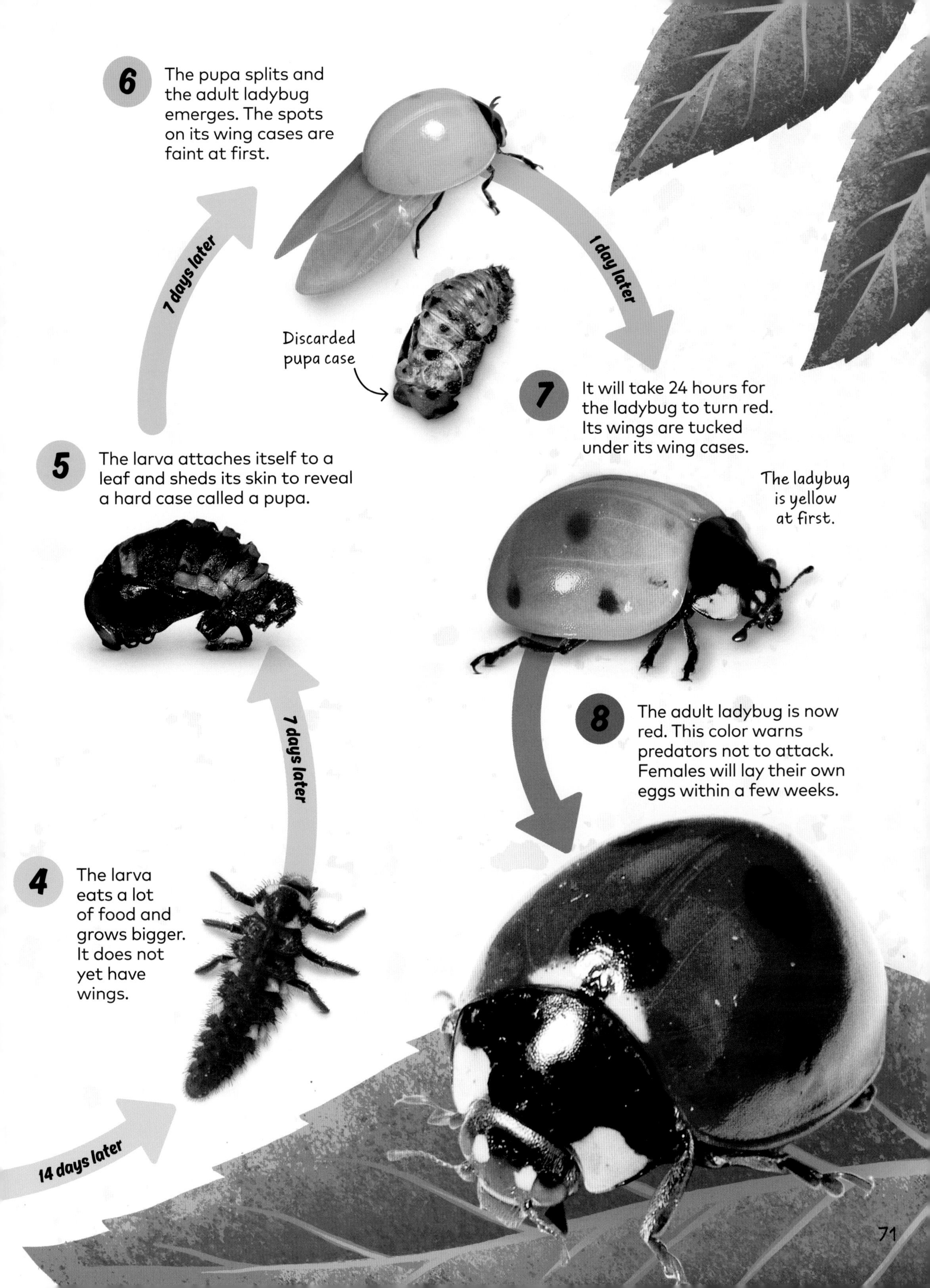
6
The pupa splits and the adult ladybug emerges. The spots on its wing cases are faint at first.
7 days later
1 day later
Discarded pupa case
7
It will take 24 hours for the ladybug to turn red. Its wings are tucked under its wing cases.
5
The larva attaches itself to a leaf and sheds its skin to reveal a hard case called a pupa.
The ladybug is yellow at first.
8
The adult ladybug is now red. This color warns predators not to attack. Females will lay their own eggs within a few weeks.
7 days later
4
The larva eats a lot of food and grows bigger. It does not yet have wings.
14 days later

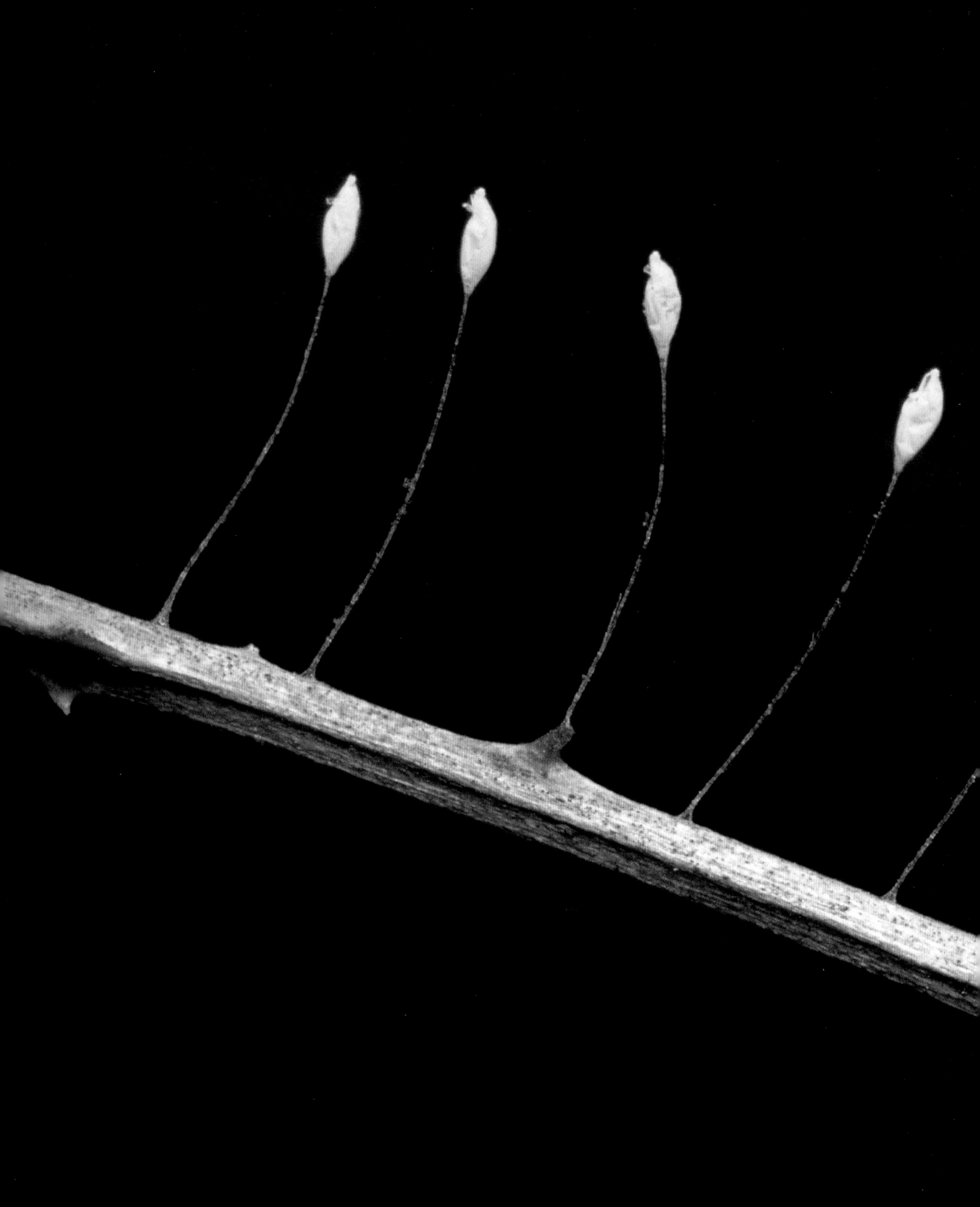

Eggs on stalks

Lacewings are a type of flying insect. A single female may lay up to 200 tiny eggs. Each egg sits at the top of a stalk. This helps to keep them out of the way of ants that may eat them.

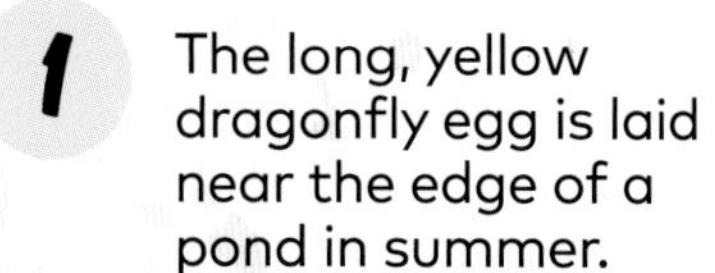

1 The long, yellow dragonfly egg is laid near the edge of a pond in summer.

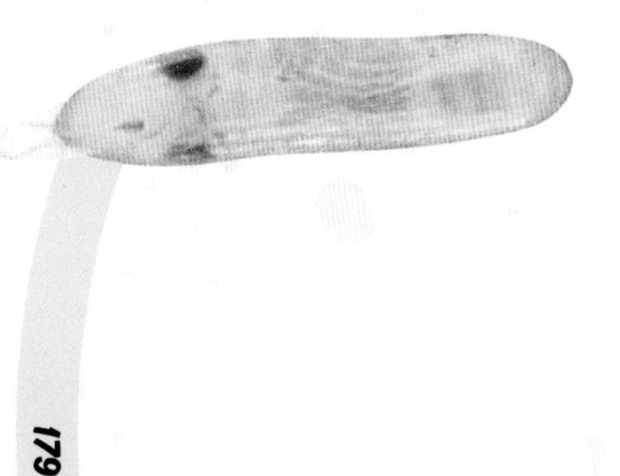

179 days later

2 The baby dragonfly, called a nymph, hatches out and moves into the water. It breathes using gills.

10 days later

3 The nymph crawls around at the bottom of the pond and hunts other small pond animals.

The nymph has a row of stripes on its body.

175 days later

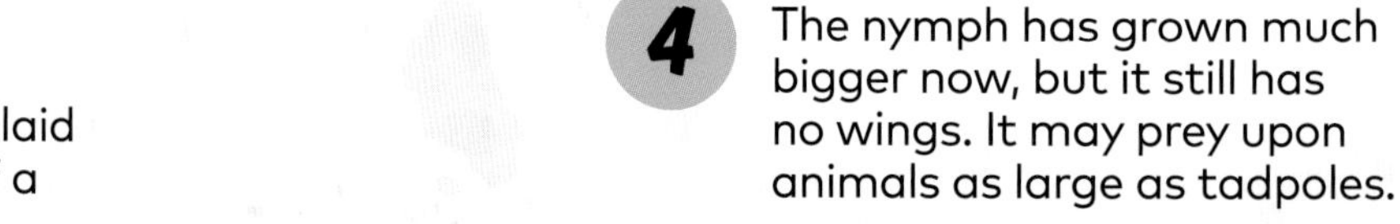

4 The nymph has grown much bigger now, but it still has no wings. It may prey upon animals as large as tadpoles.

319 days lat

Southern hawker dragonfly

Hawkers are a family of dragonflies that can be found in Europe and North America. They are some of the largest dragonflies in the world. Dragonfly eggs must be laid in or near water, which is why the adults can be found near lakes and ponds at breeding time. Male southern hawkers zoom around and fight each other for the best territories.

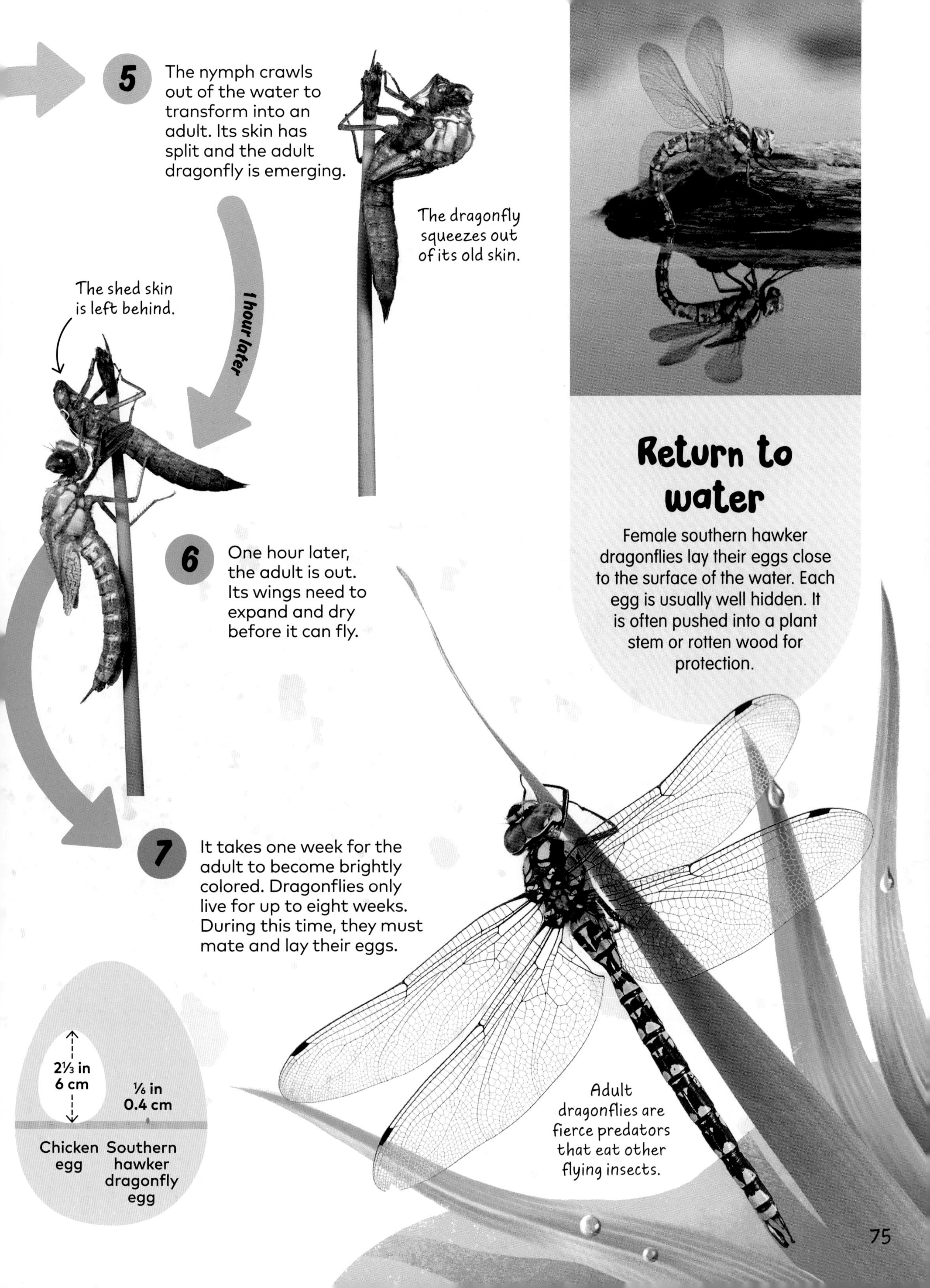

5 The nymph crawls out of the water to transform into an adult. Its skin has split and the adult dragonfly is emerging.

The dragonfly squeezes out of its old skin.

1 hour later

The shed skin is left behind.

6 One hour later, the adult is out. Its wings need to expand and dry before it can fly.

7 It takes one week for the adult to become brightly colored. Dragonflies only live for up to eight weeks. During this time, they must mate and lay their eggs.

Return to water

Female southern hawker dragonflies lay their eggs close to the surface of the water. Each egg is usually well hidden. It is often pushed into a plant stem or rotten wood for protection.

Adult dragonflies are fierce predators that eat other flying insects.

Insect eggs

They may be small, but insect eggs come in a wonderful variety of shapes and colors. Like bird eggs, insect eggs are encased in a hard shell that stops them from drying out. Females usually lay their eggs in safe places where there is plenty of food, since most insects do not look after their young.

Colorado beetle

Female Colorado beetles can lay up to 500 of these rugby-ball-shaped orange eggs. The adults and larvae eat plants and can be a pest.

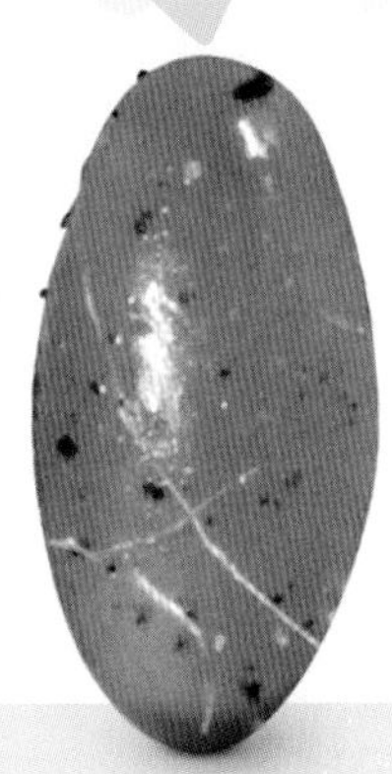

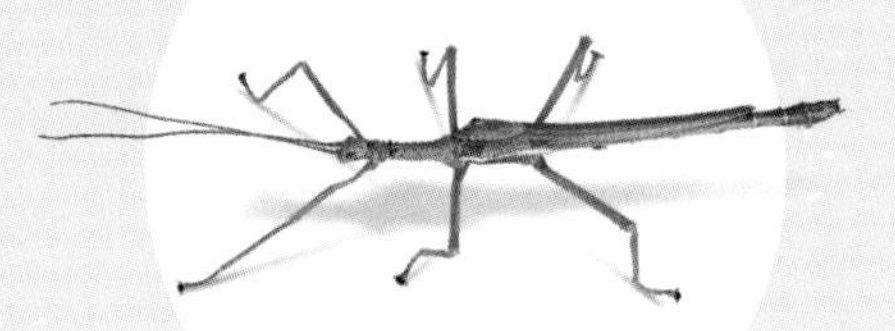

Jungle nymph

These large stick insects live in rainforests in Malaysia. Their eggs are around ⅓ in (0.8 cm) long and are laid individually in the soil.

Periphetes stick insect

Many stick insects lay intricate eggs, including this Indonesian species. The eggs look like seeds, so ants carry them underground where it is safer.

Two-spotted assassin

This predator stabs other insects with its sharp mouthparts. The nymphs that hatch from its eggs are bright red with yellow legs.

Harlequin cabbage bug

This bug's eggs look like black-and-white striped barrels. The female often lays her clutch of 12 eggs in two neat rows.

Large white butterfly

The large white butterfly likes to lay its long, yellow eggs in clusters on cabbage plants. The leaves are a favorite food of its caterpillars.

Viceroy butterfly

Viceroy butterflies lay their eggs on trees, including willow, poplar, and aspen. The spiky eggshell will be the caterpillar's first food.

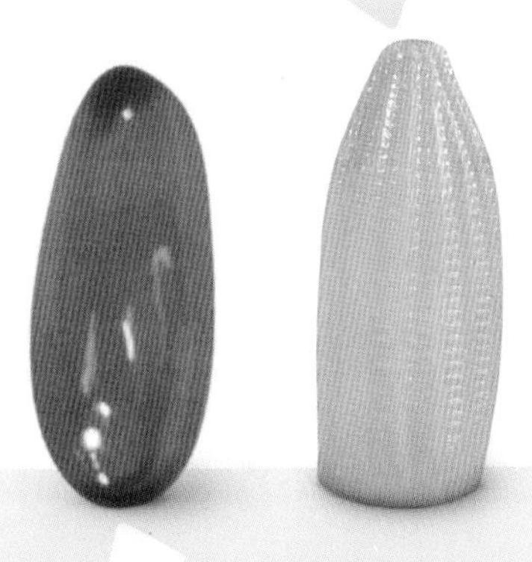

Western honey bee

A honey bee queen lays more than 2,000 eggs each day! They are kept safe in six-sided cells made from wax in the bees' nest.

Red lily beetle

The lily beetle's orange eggs are usually found on the underside of lily plant leaves. They take around a week to hatch into larvae.

Melon fly

Melon flies lay their pale eggs under the skin of many fruit, such as melons and squashes. The larvae burrow through the fruit, making it rot.

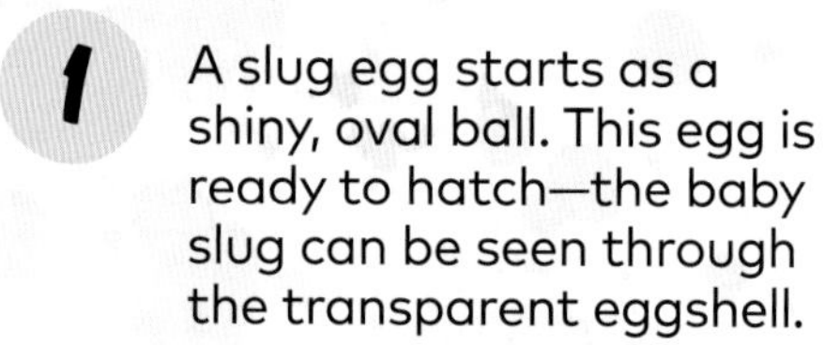

1 A slug egg starts as a shiny, oval ball. This egg is ready to hatch—the baby slug can be seen through the transparent eggshell.

The pattern on the baby slug's skin is visible inside the egg.

2 The egg hatches six weeks after it was laid. The slug starts to push itself through the hard eggshell.

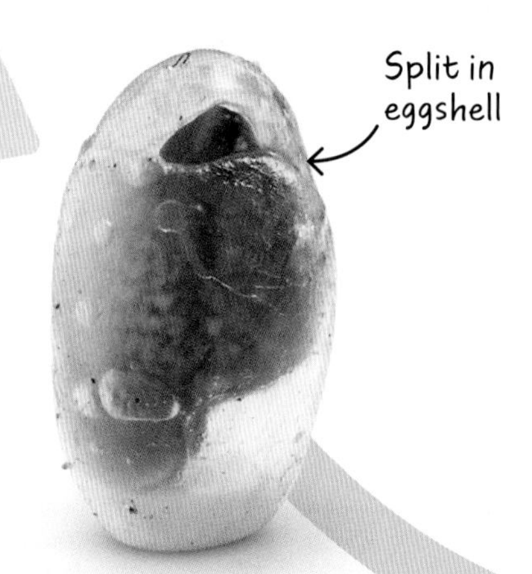

Kerry slug

2⅓ in
6 cm

⅕ in
0.5 cm

Chicken egg

Kerry slug egg

Slugs live in damp places and are active mostly at night. They feed on plants, which they scrape with their rough tongues. The Kerry slug lays around 80 eggs in total, in small batches over two to three months. The eggs are laid in holes in the ground or under rotting logs so that they stay moist because they will die if they dry out.

In danger

Slugs are like snails without shells. In fact, they do have tiny shells hidden under their skin. Without a large shell to protect it, the Kerry slug curls up into a tight ball if it is attacked.

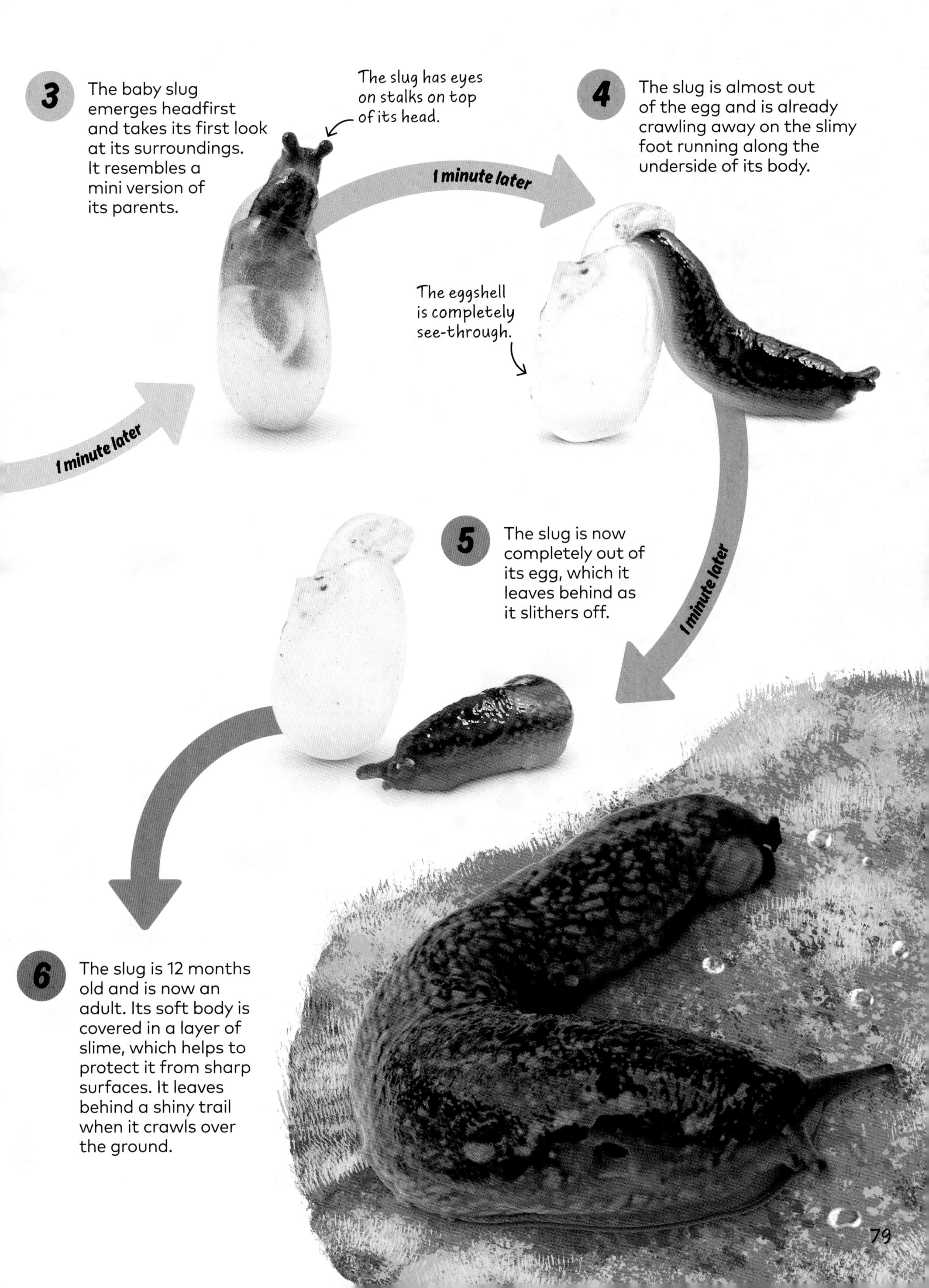
3
The baby slug emerges headfirst and takes its first look at its surroundings. It resembles a mini version of its parents.
The slug has eyes on stalks on top of its head.
1 minute later
4
The slug is almost out of the egg and is already crawling away on the slimy foot running along the underside of its body.
The eggshell is completely see-through.
1 minute later
1 minute later
5
The slug is now completely out of its egg, which it leaves behind as it slithers off.
6
The slug is 12 months old and is now an adult. Its soft body is covered in a layer of slime, which helps to protect it from sharp surfaces. It leaves behind a shiny trail when it crawls over the ground.

Index

Glossary

albumen "white" around the yolk of an egg. It helps to protect the embryo

amnion water-filled membrane that encloses an embryo

brood group of young animals that hatch at the same time from the same clutch of eggs

camouflage colors and patterns that make eggs and animals hard to see because they blend with the surroundings

cell unit that makes up all living things

clutch group of eggs that an animal lays at the same time

crèche group of young animals from several families that are guarded by only a few of their parents

down baby bird's first fluffy covering. Most of the down is replaced by thicker feathers when the bird grows up

egg lining thin, soft layer inside the eggshell

egg tooth hard lump on the tip of the beak or nose of some baby animals, which helps them to break the eggshell from the inside

eggshell outer layer of an egg, which can be hard or soft

embryo baby animal while it is developing inside the egg

fertilization joining of the male sperm with the female egg, so that the egg can start to develop into an embryo

hatching when baby animals break out of their egg

incubation period of time from when an egg starts to develop to when it hatches. Bird eggs are kept warm by their parents during this period

larva type of young stage of an insect and some other animals, when it looks quite different from its parents

membrane thin sheet of living tissue

nestling baby bird that is being looked after in the nest

nymph type of young stage of an insect when it looks like a small, wingless version of its parents

ovary organ in the female's body where eggs are made

pip first break in the eggshell made from the inside of the egg by the baby animal

pupa stage in the life of an insect during which a larva turns into an adult

yolk sac inside the egg that contains food for nourishing the embryo

Acknowledgments

DK would like to thank: Kathleen Teece for editorial assistance; Holly Price and Sonny Flynn for design assistance; Bilal Ahmed and Mohd Rizwan for hi-res work; and Caroline Hunt for proofreading.
DK would like to thank the following people and organizations for supplying some of the animals photographed in this book: Ivan Lang of Arundel Wildfowl & Wetlands Trust, Hennie Fenwick of the British Chelonia Group, Dr. Mike Majerus, Kay Medlock, Elizabeth Platt, Brighton Sealife Centre, Duncton Mill Hatchery, Tisbury Fish Farms, and the Reptile-arium, Enfield.
Additional photography by: Neil Fletcher, Geoff Brightling, Frank Greenaway, Jerry Young, Cyril Laubscher, and Harry Taylor.
Jane Burton and Kim Taylor would like to thank: Rob Harvey of Birdworld, Farnham, Surrey, for the ostrich, Humboldt penguin and crowned plover eggs; Mrs. Fleur Douetil and Roy Scholey of Busbridge Lakes, Godalming, Surrey, for the Roman goose and black swan eggs; Michael Woods for the golden pheasant and Aylesbury duck eggs; Ashmere Fisheries, Shepperton, for the quail egg, and Robert Goodden of Worldwide Butterflies, Sherbourne, Dorset, for the butterfly egg.
All other species are from the Burton-Taylor aviaries and garden. The incubators used were from A.B. Incubators Ltd., Stowmarket, Suffolk.

The publisher would like to thank the following for their kind permission to reproduce their photographs:

(Key: a-above; b-below/bottom; c-center; f-far; l-left; r-right; t-top)

4 Alamy Stock Photo: Nature Photographers Ltd / Paul R. Sterry (cra). **5 Dorling Kindersley:** Natural History Museum, London (bc). **6 123RF.com:** NewAge (tl). **Alamy Stock Photo:** Nature Photographers Ltd / Paul R. Sterry (cr); Nature Picture Library / Niall Benvie (bl). **7 Dreamstime.com:** Rudmer Zwerver / Creativenature1 (cla); Michael Elliott (b). **8 Dreamstime.com:** Jakapan Kammanern (crb); Prapass Wannapinij (clb). **9 Alamy Stock Photo:** Biosphoto / Aqua Press (clb); Lazydays Liz (cla); Ernie Janes (cra); Natural History Archive (crb). **12 Dreamstime.com:** Artushfoto (bl). **15 Dreamstime.com:** Miloslav Frybort (tr). **17 Dreamstime.com:** Dennis Jacobsen (tr). **18 Dorling Kindersley:** Chris Gomersall Photography (crb); Natural History Museum, London (c, cl, c/black). **Dreamstime.com:** Awcnz62 (clb); Brian Scantlebury (cr). **Getty Images / iStock:** Gerald Corsi (cra). **19 Alamy Stock Photo:** David Tipling Photo Library (cl, clb); Nature Photographers Ltd / Paul R. Sterry (c); Science History Images / Photo Researchers (fcr); Imagebroker / Arco Images / Pfeiffer, J. (cr). **Dreamstime.com:** Isselee (cb, c/green); Petar Kremenarov (cra); Max5128 (crb); Mikelane45 (ca). **21 Dreamstime.com:** Daniel Prudek (tr). **23 Dreamstime.com:** Karen Appleyard (br). **24 Dreamstime.com:** Charles Sichel-outcalt (bl). **26 Dreamstime.com:** Agustín Orduña Castillo (bl). **29 Alamy Stock Photo:** Vikki Martin (bl). **30-31 Alamy Stock Photo:** Buiten-Beeld / Wil Meinderts. **33 Alamy Stock Photo:** Nature Picture Library / Tui De Roy (br). **35 Alamy Stock Photo:** blickwinkel (tr). **36 Getty Images / iStock:** Andyworks (bl). **39 Alamy Stock Photo:** Peter Moulton (tr). **40 Alamy Stock Photo:** Brian Gadsby (bl). **43 123RF.com:** fotocorn (tr). **45 Alamy Stock Photo:** mauritius images GmbH / ClickAlps (br). **46-47 Dreamstime.com:** Feng Yu. **48 Alamy Stock Photo:** imageBROKER / Nigel Dennis (bl). **51 Alamy Stock Photo:** John Cancalosi (tr). **52 Dreamstime.com:** Landshark1 (bl). **54 Shutterstock.com:** Henri Koskinen (cl). **55 Dreamstime.com:** Rudmer Zwerver / Creativenature1 (b); Isselee (c). **56 Alamy Stock Photo:** Avalon.red / Andy Newman (bl). **58-59 Alamy Stock Photo:** Nature Picture Library / Remi Masson. **61 Alamy Stock Photo:** blickwinkel / Hartl (br). **62 Alamy Stock Photo:** Wil Meinderts / Buiten-beeld / Minden Pictures (bl). **64 Alamy Stock Photo:** Nature Picture Library / Adrian Davies (cl). **66 Alamy Stock Photo:** agefotostock / Marevision (cr); Mark Conlin / VWPics (cla); RGB Ventures / SuperStock / Stuart Westmorland (ca); David Fleetham (c); Mark Conlin (c/shark egg); Nature Photographers Ltd / Paul R. Sterry (crb). **Dreamstime.com:** Slowmotiongli (cl). **67 Alamy Stock Photo:** blickwinkel / Hartl (ca, c, cr); Jeff Mondragon (cla/Sockeye); Juniors Bildarchiv GmbH / Fiedler, W. / juniors@wildlife (ca/Pike); Design Pics Inc / Thomas Kline / Alaska Stock (cla); Nature Picture Library / Alex Hyde (cra); blickwinkel / A. Hartl (cl, clb). **Dreamstime.com:** Mikhailg (cb); Rostislav Stefanek (crb). **68 Alamy Stock Photo:** imageBROKER / Siepmann (tl). **69 123RF.com:** Mirosäaw Kijewski (br). **70 Getty Images / iStock:** Henrik_L (bl). **Getty Images:** Stone / Paul Starosta (cr). **71 Dreamstime.com:** Jorge Ortiz (tc). **72-73 Alamy Stock Photo:** Avalon.red / Stephen Dalton. **75 Alamy Stock Photo:** Malcolm Schuyl (tr). **76 Alamy Stock Photo:** Nature Picture Library / John Abbott (crb). **Depositphotos Inc:** lifeonwhite (c/stick egg). **Dreamstime.com:** Sarah2 (cra); Andrei Shupilo (cr). **naturepl.com:** John Abbott (c). **77 Alamy Stock Photo:** EyeEm / Aep Saepudin (crb); Nature Picture Library (cla, c/yellow); WILDLIFE GmbH (fcl). **Dorling Kindersley:** Gyuri Csoka Cyorgy (cb); Natural History Museum, London (cra, ca). **Dreamstime.com:** Alle (clb); Chrisp543 (c); Lamvanlinh93 (cr); Pimmimemom (fcr). **Science Photo Library:** US Geological Survey (cl). **78 Alamy Stock Photo:** Avalon.red / Robert Thompson (bl)

Cover images: *Front:* **Alamy Stock Photo:** imageBROKER / Herbert Kehrer cr; **Dreamstime.com:** Dibrova cb, Isselee clb, br, Kostya Pazyuk cla